"I highly recommend this book for all teachers an[d] teaching for more than thirty years and cutting is among teens. I've seen many of my students struggle with this disorder. The problem is I haven't found a reliable form of therapy for this disorder. Luckily, this book will help. It is based on dialectical behavior therapy (DBT) skills, and provides solutions and easy-to-follow strategies for those with self-harming tendencies."

—**Jackson Yee, MA**, middle school teacher

"Inflicting physical pain to release emotional pain can have debilitating effects on a teen's life. With unparalleled expertise in DBT, Sheri gives you an easy-to-follow guide that enables readers to assess problematic coping patterns, and challenge self-harming behaviors in meaningful and lasting ways. Detailed examples validate personal experiences and demonstrate how to implement skills to reduce suffering."

—**Shivani V. Gupta MSW, RSW**, clinical director at
Oakridges Therapy Centre in Richmond Hill, ON, Canada

"This warm, easy-to-understand workbook takes readers on a journey to understand why they may engage in self-harming behaviors, and teaches them healthier alternatives to manage their emotions. Sheri Van Dijk breaks down the practical strategies and skills offered in this workbook in a compassionate, nonjudgmental way. An essential tool for any teen struggling with self-harm!"

—**Maggie Mullen, LCSW**, culturally responsive social worker,
national trainer, and author of *The Dialectical Behavior Therapy
Skills Workbook for Psychosis*

"In this engaging workbook, Van Dijk provides teens who self-harm with invaluable guidance on key DBT skills. The workbook will resonate with teens through vivid and youth-relevant examples, engaging exercises, and a clear and creative way of organizing and presenting the DBT skills. Teens will find wise guidance not only on how to overcome self-harm, but more importantly, how to build a life worth living. I strongly recommend this workbook for teens who struggle with self-harm."

> —**Alexander L. Chapman, PhD, RPsych**, professor of psychology at Simon Fraser University, president of the DBT Centre of Vancouver, and coauthor of *The Borderline Personality Disorder Survival Guide*

"Sheri Van Dijk has done it again! This informative and practical book will be invaluable in helping people to understand why they engage in self-harming behaviors, and how they can use DBT skills to develop alternative responses to their emotional distress."

> —**Greg Samuelson**, registered nurse and registered psychotherapist practicing in Ontario, Canada; and founding member of the Canadian Network for Compassion Focused Therapy

"This workbook provides an easy-to-use tool for teens engaging in self-harming and self-destructive behaviors. Parents, clinicians, and others within a teen's circle of care will also benefit from the psychoeducation this book holds. The workbook uses teen-friendly language, illuminating stories, and engaging activities to explore healthier patterns of behavior. Used on its own or in addition to psychotherapy, this provides an excellent option for teens looking to improve well-being."

> —**Michelle Brans, MA**, registered psychotherapist with the Ontario College of Psychotherapists; clinical director of Counting Butterflies Child, Youth and Family Wellness; and psychotherapist in private practice specializing in teenage and emerging adult mental well-being

"Sheri Van Dijk does a wonderful job explaining self-harming and self-destructive behaviors in non-shaming ways. She starts the book by saying that people engage in these behaviors for valid reasons—they want to cope with painful experiences and emotions. However, we soon learn that there are more healthy and effective ways to deal with difficulties and pain. This book is well written and accessible for teens (and adults) who want to work through the skill-building exercises on their own or with a therapist. This workbook is helpful for those dealing with difficult life situations and painful emotions so they can live a healthier life."

—**Karma Guindon, PhD, RSW, CCFT**, psychotherapist, consultant, and educator in private practice in Bolton and Newmarket, ON, Canada

"Sheri does an exceptional job of outlining valuable skills; and describes a way for the reader to incorporate them into their lives. We can lose the power of a message with complicating theories and in-depth explanations. Sheri has managed to demonstrate incredible acceptance and validation, with positive and accessible directions for change; and she does so beautifully in print form. Within the learning and choices offered here, there is an invitation to pause and consider the options available. Well suited in both her choice of language, and balancing both text and worksheets. This workbook offers a path to recover from unhealthy coping, while learning how to emotionally regulate."

—**Leanne M. Garfinkel, MA, SEP**, registered psychotherapist (CRPO)

the dbt skills workbook for teen self-harm

practical tools to help you manage emotions & overcome self-harming behaviors

SHERI VAN DIJK, MSW

Instant Help Books
An Imprint of New Harbinger Publications, Inc.

Publisher's Note

Distributed in Canada by Raincoast Books

Copyright © 2021 by Sheri Van Dijk
      Instant Help Books
      An imprint of New Harbinger Publications, Inc.
      5674 Shattuck Avenue
      Oakland, CA 94609
      www.newharbinger.com

INSTANT HELP, the Clock Logo, and NEW HARBINGER are trademarks of New Harbinger Publications, Inc.

Cover design by Amy Shoup

Acquired by Tesilya Hanauer

Edited by Karen Schader

All Rights Reserved

Library of Congress Cataloging-in-Publication Data on file

Book printed in the United States of America

24   23   22

10   9   8   7   6   5   4   3   2

Firstly, this book is dedicated to my clients: thank you for allowing me to be a part of your journey and to be witness to the positive changes you've had the courage to make!

I would also like to dedicate this book to my family: Mom and Dad, Lisa, Roop, Caleb, Makenna, Jim, and Tess and Oliver. Thank you for always being there to support me. I love you all.

Contents

Introduction   1

1   What Is Self-Harm, and Why Do You Do It?   5

2   Surviving the Crisis   21

3   How to Get Your Groove On   37

4   Finding Your Internal Wisdom   49

5   Name the Feeling to Tame It   63

6   Stop Adding Fuel to the Fire   81

7   Avoid Avoiding   103

8   The Importance of Relationships   125

Conclusion: Where Are You Now?   147

References   155

Introduction

You may already know that a lot of people self-harm—deliberately cause injury to their body—so no, you're not crazy, you're not weird. There are actually many understandable reasons why people hurt themselves in different ways. But there's at least a part of you that also recognizes this isn't healthy or effective in the long term, or you probably wouldn't be reading these words. So, first of all, thank you for picking up this book, and congratulations for recognizing that self-harm isn't something you want to keep in your life in the long run.

The first goal of this book is to help you understand your behavior, whether it's actually doing something to physically injure your body, like cutting or burning yourself, or doing something that's self-destructive, like abusing drugs or alcohol or having unprotected sex with people you don't know. The second goal is to teach you skills to help you deal with the things in your life that are causing you to turn to these unhealthy ways of coping with your pain and the hard stuff life throws at you.

This book is based on a treatment called dialectical behavior therapy (DBT), which was created by Dr. Marsha Linehan (1993), a psychologist in the United States. Her goal was to help people just like yourself, struggling with self-harming behaviors and urges, and even those who have thoughts of suicide. This workbook will teach you the skills you need to help you live a healthier life, where you'll be able to make choices for yourself and have relationships with others that you'll feel good about. Over time, healthier choices and positive relationships will help you start to feel better about yourself; in the long run, this usually helps people see that self-harming isn't something they want in their lives and helps them eliminate these behaviors.

The skills you'll learn in this book fall into four categories. *Crisis survival skills* will help you survive the crisis—whatever it may be—without making things worse for yourself. *Core mindfulness skills* will help you reduce the emotional pain you're feeling, and not act on urges, as you begin to live more in the present moment and become more accepting of things in your life. *Emotion regulation skills* will teach you more about emotions and how to manage them in healthier ways. And *interpersonal effectiveness skills* will help you have more balanced and satisfying relationships with others. By doing the activities in this workbook, you'll learn more about these skills and how to use them. Some worksheets are also available for download at the website for this book: http://www.newharbinger.com/45458. (See the very back of this book for more details.)

Why do some of us turn to self-harming and self-destructive behaviors in the first place? There's a lot yet to be learned about our brains, and when it comes to emotions, there's still a lot of work to do, but in DBT we believe that people who turn to these behaviors do so because of two things. First, some who turn to these behaviors are born with a higher level of sensitivity than others. Is this you? Do you feel things more often and more intensely than others? Do people tell you that you're "overreacting" to things? That you're full of "drama"? If this sounds like you, rest assured that you've done nothing to cause this! This higher level of sensitivity can be related to genes inherited from your parents; it may be related to a mental health condition you were born with; or it can be because of problems your mom had while she was pregnant. (And no, we're not blaming your mom, either! But if she had physical or mental health problems or experienced some kind of trauma or high stress while she was pregnant, for example, this could have had an effect on your development.) BTW, it's also important to know that being more sensitive isn't all bad; while it might mean more pain at times, more sensitive people are usually also the more creative and passionate people, and you tend to form more intense connections with others because of your ability to feel things so deeply.

But this is just one part of the story of why people may turn to self-harming and self-destructive behaviors; the other part is the environment you grow up in. Our environment plays a large role in our development, and for people who turn to these kinds of behaviors, trauma is a common experience, such as having been abused or neglected in some way. But you don't have to have experienced abuse to turn to problematic behaviors. In DBT, we believe that one of the most common environmental factors that contributes to people turning to self-harming and self-destructive behaviors is growing up in an *invalidating environment*, an environment in which you were taught that your internal experiences (like your emotions and your thoughts) were wrong.

While none of us lives in a world where our emotions, thoughts, and beliefs are always understood and accepted, some people grow up in environments where they regularly receive the message that there's something wrong with them—this, combined with high sensitivity, is what often leads to self-harming and self-destructive behaviors. The takeaway here is that it's not your fault that you've developed the problems you have that have led to self-harming or self-destructive behaviors. It's the combination of your sensitivity and the environment you've grown up in that, for whatever reason, wasn't able to give you what you needed emotionally. So no, it's not your fault, and yes, it's still up to you to work to make things better for yourself!

In the next chapter, I'll talk more about self-harm and self-destructive behaviors to give you a better understanding of these problems and how this book will help you with them. Then you'll learn some skills that can take the place of those behaviors over time, to make it more likely that you'll be able to deal with the difficult things that happen in your life (and the painful feelings that come up as a result) without these behaviors. If you choose to continue to read—and I hope you will!—it's important to remember that change doesn't happen overnight. Do some thinking about what you've already learned here. In chapter 1, you'll have an opportunity to think more about how ready and willing you are to do this difficult, but very rewarding and worthwhile, work. Good luck. I hope you stick with me!

Chapter 1

What Is Self-Harm, and Why Do You Do It?

Self-harm refers to deliberately inflicting injury on your body in some way with the intention of hurting yourself but without intending to kill yourself. The most common ways of self-harming are cutting, hitting, punching, or burning yourself, although there are many other ways that people self-harm. Sometimes people who self-harm have a mental health problem such as depression or anxiety, but many people without these problems also self-harm.

There are also behaviors that we can think of as *self-destructive*, where you're doing damage to your life in some way—for example, disordered eating behaviors like making yourself throw up or not eating; or abusing drugs or alcohol—but you're not causing direct harm to your body. This is an important difference for you to know about, because people who self-harm have a much higher risk for taking this behavior further and trying to kill themselves. Both self-harm and self-destructive behaviors are obviously problematic, though, and people who self-harm tend to do self-destructive things as well, so there's often a lot of overlap between the two.

There's also overlap in where these problems stem from: more sensitive people who have grown up in invalidating environments often don't learn how to handle their emotions in healthy ways. This is what's often called *emotion dysregulation*. If you've never learned skillful ways of managing your emotions, it's understandable that you'll turn to different things to try to turn the pain off—like cutting and other forms of self-harm or substance abuse and other forms of self-destructive behaviors.

The skills you'll learn in this book will help you eliminate both self-harming and self-destructive behaviors by giving you some healthier ways of managing emotions. To understand these ideas a bit better, do the following activity to consider what self-harming or self-destructive behaviors you turn to in your life. From now on, I'll refer to these behaviors as your *target behaviors*.

Activity: What Are Your Target Behaviors?

Review the following list and check off the behaviors that you've done in the past twelve months:

Self-Harm Behaviors:

☐ Cutting   ☐ Punching/hitting

☐ Ingesting dangerous substances   ☐ Puncturing

☐ Extreme scratching   ☐ Biting

☐ Interference with wound-healing   ☐ Extreme skin-picking

☐ Burning   ☐ Head-banging

☐ Pinching   ☐ Breaking bones

Other:_____

Other:_____

Self-Destructive Behaviors:

☐ Self-induced vomiting   ☐ Restricting eating

☐ Bingeing   ☐ Using recreational drugs

☐ Abusing alcohol   ☐ Hair pulling

☐ Misusing over-the-counter meds   ☐ Gambling

☐ Video gaming excessively   ☐ Lying

☐ Stealing

☐ Watching pornography excessively

☐ Shoplifting

☐ Excessively using social media

☐ Vaping

☐ Overspending

☐ Engaging in unprotected sex

☐ Driving dangerously

☐ Sexting

☐ Smoking

☐ Sleeping to avoid

☐ Being aggressive toward others

☐ Bullying others

Other:_____

Other:_____

Now that you have a better understanding of whether your target behaviors are self-harming or self-destructive—and what your target behaviors are—let's look at some of the reasons you might be doing these things.

Why Self-Harm?

When you don't grow up learning healthy ways of dealing with emotions, you can learn to avoid emotions through self-harming or self-destructive behaviors. It makes sense. Of course, just because it makes sense doesn't mean we want it to stay this way! But understanding and accepting yourself without judgment is important. The following story shows an example of how self-harming behaviors may develop.

Connor's Story

Connor's father was a police officer, and he grew up looking up to his father and admiring how strong he was. His dad never seemed to be afraid of anything, and nothing ever seemed to bother him. Even when his grandpa died when Connor was eight, he didn't see his dad cry. He wanted to be just like him, but Connor knew he wasn't like his dad: he seemed to feel things more, and he would get really sad even just watching a movie. He didn't want to be this way, but he didn't know what to do about it.

Connor's parents separated when he was twelve, and his dad moved out of the house. Connor was devastated, but he knew he had to be strong; his dad even reminded him that he had to take care of his younger brother now that he wouldn't be living at home with them anymore. Connor's sadness and fear got really intense at times, but he knew he couldn't let others know how he was feeling—he had to be strong for both his parents. When Connor was fourteen, his friend told him that he had cut himself on purpose when he had been feeling really angry about something. Although it sounded strange to Connor—how on earth could cutting himself make him feel better?—he was desperate one night when he was feeling really sad and decided to give it a try. What he found was that cutting helped him to not feel his feelings for a while. This was such a huge relief for him, even for just a few hours, that he began turning to this more and more often. He had discovered that, with cutting, he didn't have to feel the feelings.

You might find yourself struggling to figure out why you use your target behavior or behaviors. When you've been doing something for a long time, it's easy to lose the ability to think objectively about it and see it for what it really is (and what it does for you).

Activity: What Does Your Target Behavior Do for You?

Think about your target behavior (if you identified more than one target behavior in the previous activity, pick one to think about). Now look through the following list and check off the reasons you think you do that behavior.

Your target behavior:

☐ Creates some kind of pleasurable emotion (like peace, calm, or even joy or euphoria)

☐ Helps to manage intense emotions

☐ Communicates to others that you need help

☐ Provides relief from your current situation or emotion

☐ Proves that you're not invisible

☐ Makes you feel in control

☐ Distracts from emotional pain

☐ Lets you feel something other than numb

☐ Is a way of punishing yourself

☐ Validates the emotional pain you're feeling

☐ Is an attempt to change the behavior of others

☐ Shows your desperation to others (it's proof of how bad things are)

☐ Helps you avoid or escape painful feelings

☐ Is a way of avoiding suicide

Add any other reasons you can think of:

_____

_____

Now that you're more aware of some of the reasons you do this behavior, it can be helpful to look at the positive and negative consequences of doing it. Many of us tend to be more aware of the negative consequences of our behaviors, especially when we know these behaviors are unhealthy. Recognizing the positives along with the negatives, however, can help you understand what keeps it going as well as consider the reasons you want to stop it. It can also help you decide if you're ready to commit to making a change. It takes a lot of energy and effort to make these kinds of changes, and you won't get very far if you're not truly committed. You might be feeling anxious just thinking about the possibility of getting rid of your target behavior. It's like an old blanket, providing a sense of comfort and security even though it's worn, full of holes, and doesn't actually keep you warm anymore—the difference being, of course, that an old blanket isn't actually going to be harmful to you!

The next activity will help you examine the pros and cons of your target behavior (Linehan 2014). Before you begin, take a look at how Connor completed this activity. Connor wrote down all the pros and cons for cutting and for not cutting in the following chart. Connor then rated each pro and con on a scale of 1 (least important) to 3 (most important). He then totaled the results.

SAMPLE WORKSHEET: CONNOR'S PROS AND CONS OF CUTTING

Pros of Cutting	Cons of Cutting
It gives me immediate relief from emotions (3) *Distracts me from my feelings* (3) *Seeing the cut/blood makes my feelings seem more real* (2) Total: 8	*I feel guilt and shame afterward* (3) *It stops me from finding other ways of dealing with things* (3) *I have to hide my cuts and scars from everyone* (2) *I'm constantly afraid my parents are going to find out* (3) *If people find out, I might lose my job coaching kids' soccer* (3) Total: 14
Pros of Not Cutting	**Cons of Not Cutting**
I feel better about myself (3) *No cuts or scars to hide* (2) *No fear about people finding out* (3) *My parents will be proud of me* (2) *It forces me to deal with things in healthier ways* (2) Total: 12	*It's really hard!* (2) *There's no immediate relief* (3) *I have to learn other ways of dealing with stuff* (2) *It's scary to think of not having this to help me deal with pain* (2) *I'm afraid I might do something worse instead* (1) Total: 10

When Connor added the pros of cutting (8) to the cons of not cutting (10), he came up with a total of 18. This number was lower than the cons of cutting (14) plus the pros of not cutting (12), which came to 26. In other words, the negatives of cutting outweighed the positives. Sometimes having this number can be even more helpful than just writing out the pros and cons.

Activity: What Are the Consequences?

Now it's your turn. First, fill in the blank line at the top of each quadrant with the target behavior that you are examining.

1. Under pros of doing this target behavior, write down any positive consequences that come to mind. What are the good things that result from this behavior? What do you get out of it? Why is it hard to let it go?

2. Under cons of doing this target behavior, write down the negative consequences. What problems does it cause? Why are you considering letting go of it?

3. Now, under pros of not doing this behavior, write down the positives of working to reduce or eliminate this target behavior. Why would it be a good thing if you were no longer hurting yourself in this way?

4. Finally, under cons of not doing this behavior, write down any negatives that will result from reducing or eliminating your target behavior. How would it be a bad thing if you no longer had this behavior to turn to?

Feel free to use any responses in Connor's pros and cons chart that resonate with you. You can also refer back to the checklist from the previous activity. Most importantly, though, be sure to consider what your own truth is about what's helpful and unhelpful about your target behavior.

If you get stuck, here are some things to consider. Does your target behavior have positive or negative consequences for your relationships? Does it help you move toward your long-term and short-term goals? Does it help you or prevent you from doing certain things?

WORKSHEET: PROS AND CONS CHART

Pros of _____	Cons of _____
Pros of Not _____	**Cons of Not** _____

Hopefully, this chart has helped you consider your target behavior from a different perspective, giving you the bigger picture of both why you turn to the behavior and why you want to stop it. It's important to weigh all of the consequences when making a decision like this. It may be helpful to come back to the pros and cons of this behavior more than once, so you can be sure you're thinking about your responses from a balanced perspective instead of being ruled by the urge and by your emotions. Once you can't think of anything else to put in the chart, rate each of your responses from 1 (least important) to 3 (most important); then add up each column to get a more thorough understanding of how important the pros and cons of the behavior are.

Now ask yourself if you're ready to make a commitment to change.

Activity: Setting Your Goal

When you are ready, fill in the following statement:

My goal for myself is to (circle one):

Stop   Reduce   Other: _____

the following behavior(s): _____

If you have identified more than one target behavior, it's probably best to work on one at a time, so you won't get overwhelmed. (Visit http://www.newharbinger .com/45458 to download the pros and cons chart if you want to examine the pros and cons of other target behaviors.) By the way, just *counting* a behavior you're trying to change can actually have a positive effect on that behavior, so you may want to start keeping track of the number of times you engage in your target behavior. (You can do this without anyone knowing—keep notes in your phone in a secure folder, or put a small "x" in your agenda or day planner each time you do this behavior.)

Analyzing Your Behavior

You've already done a lot of work to understand why you resort to your target behavior, and you've identified the positive and negative consequences of this behavior—and way to go for that! But before you can effectively work on changing your behavior, you have to have a good understanding of all the different parts of it. You might think you know the ins and outs of your behavior already—and I'm sure that you understand at least some aspects of it, and maybe you even have a really good understanding of it. But quite often, there are bits and pieces that people aren't aware of, and that's why you need to do a behavioral analysis (BA) (Linehan 2014). A behavioral analysis walks through your experience of the target behavior in detail. First, have a look at Louisa's story and her BA.

Louisa's Story

Louisa had a number of target behaviors that she used to help her cope, including cutting herself, punching herself and the walls, and yelling and swearing at her family. When she was calm, she could see how much of a problem these behaviors were, and she didn't want to keep doing them, but once she started to feel a strong emotion, she would just lose control. She had been working on this in therapy for a few years but hadn't made much progress and was feeling frustrated.

When Louisa started doing BAs on her target behaviors, she realized that there was much more to them than she had previously understood, and this new information helped her start to make changes.

Sample Worksheet: Louisa's Behavioral Analysis

Date completed: Feb. 3rd   **Date of target behavior:** Feb. 3rd

Target behavior: *I cut my arm with a razor blade at 7:00 p.m. today when Conrad hadn't texted me back.*

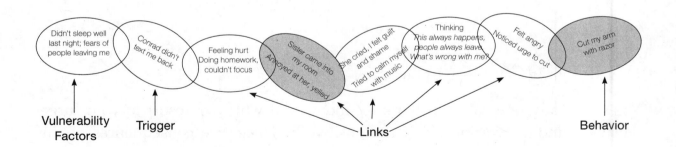

Pros of the behavior: Cons of the behavior:

Felt immediate relief   *I'm not learning to use skills*

Prevented me from feeling the hurt   *Disappointment in myself*

Helps me see my pain is real or valid   *Now I have another scar*

Activity: Behavioral Analysis

Using Louisa's example as a guide, complete a behavioral analysis on your own target behavior. Use the space provided in this workbook, or visit http://www.newharbinger .com/45458 to download copies of the behavioral analysis worksheet to use now (or in the future). Try doing the BA as soon as possible after doing your target behavior, so you can easily recall a lot of detail about the situation (along with your thoughts, feelings, and actions). While you're doing this, keep in mind that it will likely feel pretty uncomfortable, especially at first, as chances are you've never looked so closely at your behavior. It's common for people to feel shame, anxiety, anger at themselves, or other painful feelings while doing a BA, but do your best to push yourself to do it anyway, because completing the BA will help you stop doing this behavior.

First write down the target behavior that you are about to analyze. Fill in the date that you did the target behavior and the date of the analysis. Then fill in the rest of the blanks by answering the following:

1. What are your vulnerability factors? What made it more likely on this occasion that you were going to do the behavior? For example, Louisa noted she hadn't slept very well the night before. Here are some other possibilities: Were you hungry (hangry)? If you're taking medications for mental or physical health problems, had you taken your meds? If you are a girl, does your menstrual cycle make you more emotionally vulnerable? Louisa also noted a history of people leaving that led to her fear of losing people. Perhaps you've tried to talk to your parents about your feelings before and they didn't seem to understand, so you may have learned, *There's no point in talking to others*, and you tend to deal with your feelings by drinking alcohol instead.

2. What was the trigger? What event started the chain that led to the behavior? Louisa knew the trigger for her was not hearing back from her friend. If you can't put your finger on one specific event, you might be able to see that things were generally stressful in your life. (If you can't figure out the trigger, don't stress too much about it. Just try to figure out as best as you can when the urge to do the behavior first came up, and use that as a starting point.)

3. What were the links to the behavior? You can think of the links as each step in the story: what were you thinking, what were you feeling, what were you doing, and what was happening around you? Try to fill in as many details as possible, from the trigger (or from when you first noticed the urge) to when you actually did the behavior.

4. What behavior did this lead to?

WORKSHEET: BEHAVIORAL ANALYSIS

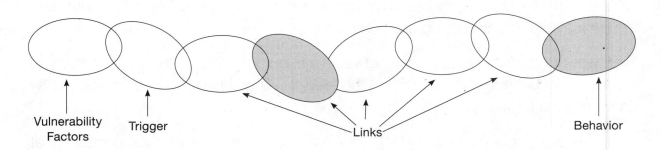

Whew! Hard work, right? Unfortunately, it does take a lot of work, energy, and effort to change most behavior. Let me assure you, though, that it won't always be this way. Right now, you need to gather data that will help you understand your behavior, the purpose it's been serving, what's been keeping it going, and so on. This is the hardest part—and it's temporary! Once you have the information that you need, you'll switch gears and begin focusing less on the behavior itself and more on what to do about it—still not easy, but it's a process. Like learning to play lacrosse or swim or how to do calculus or play a new game, it's hard work at first, but it will come more naturally over time. So please don't become discouraged!

It's best to do at least four BAs for a target behavior, analyzing the same kind of behavior on four different occasions. This will give you enough data to begin to see certain patterns among your vulnerability factors, your triggers, and the links between triggers and your behavior.

Activity: Reviewing the Data

After you have completed at least four BAs, look at them together and answer the following.

1. Is there a pattern to your vulnerability factors? Do certain things tend to make you more vulnerable? How can you address these things to reduce the likelihood that you'll act on this urge when it comes up again? For example, if lack of sleep makes you more vulnerable, you could decide that you need to work on getting more sleep by going to bed earlier, which may mean turning off your computer and phone earlier. If forgetting to take your meds causes you to be more vulnerable, you may decide to put an alarm in your cell phone as a reminder.

_____

_____

_____

2. Is there a theme behind what triggers you to do the behavior? For example, is there a person in your life whom the urge centers around? Is there a thought (such as *People always leave*) that seems to be a pattern causing problems? Is there a particular emotion that seems to be the trigger?

_____

_____

_____

3. Looking at the links to your behavior, can you see places where you might have been able to do something different to break the chain so that you wouldn't have continued down the path to the target behavior? This may be hard to figure out at this point, but you'll be able to add more ideas as you learn more skills in chapter 2. Use the space provided to write down any ideas you may have now. It could be doing a forward bend or pacing your breathing if you felt hurt; calling a crisis

line or trying to talk to your mom if you were unable to focus on your home-work; putting your face in cold water and distracting yourself in other ways if you noticed the urge to cut.

_____

_____

_____

4. Now go back and look at the consequences that you noted under pros and cons of the behavior. Look more closely at the positive consequences (what you get out of the behavior). Again, these positive consequences are why you keep doing it even when you can see this behavior is problematic. Try to look at these positive consequences objectively, without judgment. What needs does your target behavior meet, and can you think of other ways to meet those needs? For example, letting yourself cry might provide immediate relief. Talking to someone supportive might provide the validation you seem to need.

_____

_____

_____

Having a better understanding of your target behavior can help you change your behavior. It's also important to consider whether others in your life are somehow giving you something positive that's encouraging the target behavior.

Positive Reinforcements

Is someone rewarding your behavior? It's important to look at this if it's helping to keep your target behavior going. If you've ever trained a dog, you know that when you say "sit," and your dog does, you can reinforce the behavior by giving a treat, making it more likely you'll get that behavior again in the future. Humans learn the same way—we're more likely to repeat behavior if we receive positive feedback for it—so consider this. If someone in your life knows about your target behavior, how do they respond to it? Do they give you a treat? For example, when your mom finds out that you cut yourself, does she give you affection and reassurance? Does your dad take you to the doctor, demand that you speak to someone about your problems? Is there time off from school? Do your responsibilities decrease?

Even though some of these things might seem uncomfortable, they might also be much-needed reminders that people care about you, and maybe you don't get those reminders regularly unless you engage in your target behavior.

Activity: Is Someone Giving You a "Treat"?

Write down any possible treats that others are giving you when you've engaged in your target behavior.

_____

_____

_____

Now consider if there are things you could do to get your needs met without engaging in your target behavior, and write them down here. For example, you could ask someone for a hug, tell your parents you'd like to speak to a therapist, go see your guidance counselor at school, or call or text your local crisis line.

_____

_____

_____

Wrapping Up

This chapter has focused on helping you get a better understanding of the target behaviors you've been turning to. Before moving on, think about what you've learned so far. When reading about being more sensitive and experiencing invalidation, and how the combination of these things often leads to problems managing emotions, could you see where your own target behavior might have started? Are you doing other things that you didn't realize were problematic? Or maybe you have behaviors that aren't usually problematic, but you do them so often that they've turned into a problem, like video gaming or sleeping to avoid your life.

The BA is a helpful tool in developing awareness, and it's important to use it. Remember to think of this as data collection; you need as much information as possible to successfully tackle the problem. BAs take time and energy, but once you've generated a few of them, it's about looking at the information you've collected, so you can start to make changes—and, yes, those change skills are coming next!

Take your time as you continue to work through this book. Rushing through it is not going to get you anywhere, as lasting change takes effort and time. You've come this far, so I hope you'll keep going. In the next chapter, you're going to start learning some crisis survival skills that will help you to not act on the urge to do the target behavior. So, hang in there, and please turn the page.

Chapter 2

Surviving the Crisis

In time, you'll learn some skills that will help you reduce your painful feelings. But first you need to learn how to get through the crisis without making it worse by acting on the urge to do your target behavior. This chapter is about replacing the old self-harming and self-destructive behaviors with new, more skillful behaviors that won't have the same negative consequences. This will include some goal setting, to help you increase your will to change, and then you'll learn some ways to reduce the likelihood that you'll act on unhealthy urges when they do arise.

Stephanie's Story

Stephanie had started out her life in an abusive home. She learned early on that it wasn't okay to express any kind of feelings and that it was safer to stuff them all inside. This was really painful, though, and she learned that cutting herself could help her deal with that pain—it distracted her and gave her physical pain to focus on instead of the hurt she felt inside. The physical pain also made the emotional pain more real for her—it was like the cuts on her body were evidence of the emotional pain she was feeling. When she was sixteen, Stephanie decided that she wanted to help kids who were going through difficult situations similar to what she had been through, but she knew that to do this, she had to learn healthier ways of managing her own emotions. This motivated her to work to stop hurting herself, but Stephanie had been stuck in this behavior for so long that she wasn't sure how to stop.

What Are Your Goals?

Even if you aren't sure how to stop, the first step is to recognize your long-term goals. Stephanie was able to see that cutting was going to get in the way of her long-term goal of working with kids, and this motivated her to change her behavior. If you can identify a long-term goal like this—something that will make your life more worth living—you can often use it to stay on track.

Activity: Your Goals

Take some time to write down some of your long-term goals in the following space. These might include specific career goals, educational goals (finishing high school, getting into a college program), or relationship goals in terms of friends or having a significant other. They might be related to moving toward something (like better mental health or stability in your life) or moving away from something (like a difficult family member, getting out of the mental health system, or staying out of the hospital).

_____   _____

_____   _____

_____   _____

Now that you've identified some of your long-term goals, draw a picture here to represent them. If you don't like to draw, you can jot down some notes instead. Alternatively, you could get even more creative, like making a collage to represent your goals and dreams and hanging it on your bedroom wall so that you have a visual reminder of why you don't want to do your target behaviors.

It can also be useful to practice seeing yourself in the future, by envisioning yourself at your high school graduation, at college surrounded by new friends, or in your dream job. Describe the thoughts and feelings that come up for you as you see yourself in this future situation.

_____

_____

_____

The more you focus on your positive goals, the more likely you will be able to reach them. This can also take the focus off the target behavior.

Reducing the Opportunity

One way of reducing a target behavior is to reduce the opportunity to engage in that behavior, by simply taking away the available means. In other words, if you usually cut yourself in the shower with the razor you use to shave your legs, you need to take the razor out of the shower, even if it's inconvenient! If you usually burn yourself, get rid of your lighter. If drugs or alcohol is your go-to, give your stash to someone who will get rid of it for you.

If you don't have easy access to the means of doing the behavior, you'll be less likely to do it. Even if you could eventually get access to something else to hurt yourself with, this will still delay your ability to act on the urge, and that in itself can be helpful, as something might happen in the meantime that will motivate you to make a healthier choice. When you're having urges to hurt yourself or self-destruct, the important thing is to not just let yourself act on the urge.

You can get creative with your thinking about how to delay acting on the urge. I once worked with someone who was trying to stop smoking cannabis; he wasn't ready yet to get rid of his stash altogether, so instead he put it in a shoebox in the closet, under a pile of his belongings, so that he really had to work hard to get to it.

Activity: How Can You Delay?

What can you do to make it less likely that you'll act on your urge immediately? Jot your ideas down here:

_____ _____

_____ _____

Delaying your immediate response to act on an urge can give you time to do something else.

Changing Your Body's State to Manage Emotions

When the urge arises, you can change what's happening in your body to help manage your emotions. Here are some quick ways to regulate your emotions by doing something different with your body.

Forward bend. Bend over as though trying to touch your toes (no worries if you can't actually touch them, and you can do this sitting down, if easier). Take some slow, deep breaths and hang out there for a little while. Usually this helps your body feel a little calmer. Just don't stand up too quickly, or you might fall over.

Stick your face in cold water. If you're not taking a medication known as a beta-blocker and you don't have problems with low blood pressure or disordered eating (restricting or purging), putting your face in cold water is another way that can quickly get your emotions regulated (Linehan 2014). When feeling the urge to do a target behavior, instead you go to the nearest sink, fill it with cold water, and put your face in the water for as long as you can hold your breath. Alternatively, you can splash cold water on your face or hold an ice pack over your eyes, but it works best if you hold your breath and tip yourself over as though putting your face in cold water. Doing this activity two or three times will help settle your emotions fast. (If you're not sure if this is okay for you to do, be sure to check with your doctor before trying it.)

Pace your breathing. Paced breathing is another way to get your emotions back under control (Linehan 2014). Focusing on making your exhale longer than your inhale activates a system in your body that helps you slow down and feel calmer. Here's how to do this. When you inhale, count in your head to see how long your inhale is. Then, as you exhale, count at the same pace and make sure your exhale is at least a little bit longer than your inhale. For example, if you get to a count of four when you inhale, make sure you exhale to a count of at least five. Breathe this way for several minutes or until you feel yourself calming down.

Increase your heart rate through exercise. Doing some intense exercise can also help to regulate your emotions. Go for a fast run, do some jumping jacks or lunges in your bedroom, or run up and down your stairs. Intense exercise gives the chemicals in your brain a boost and helps you manage emotions.

These four ways of regulating your emotions work in the short term. I think of them as creating an opportunity to temporarily de-hijack yourself from your emotions so that you can think a little more clearly about how to help yourself not do the target behavior. This is where the next set of skills comes in.

Distracting Yourself

We've all had times when we've struggled with emotions, and even been in a crisis, and yet managed to not act on self-harming or self-destructive urges. Sometimes in difficult situations, you might find you're able to do some things that are healthy for you, like talking to someone about your struggles, going for a walk, or cuddling with your dog or cat. These distractions are examples of crisis survival skills (Linehan 2014).

Activity: How Do You Distract Yourself?

List some of the things you already do that are healthy ways of managing your emotions (for example, listening to music, taking a bath, calling a friend, or stretching):

_____

_____

While such distractions won't necessarily take your pain or the urge away, and they won't fix the problem, they will help you get through the crisis without making it worse.

Here are some other activities that many people find helpful to get their mind off a difficult situation.

- Watch something funny on TV.

- Play a sport you enjoy.

- Play a video game.

- Reach out to a friend.

- Bake yourself a treat.

- Go for a walk outside.

- Watch videos of baby animals on YouTube.

- Read a book.

- Do a jigsaw puzzle.

- Write a poem.

- Do your homework.

- Clean your room.

- Hold an ice cube in your hand.

- Organize your closet.

- Go for a run.

- Go to the gym.

- Cuddle with your dog or cat.

- Chew on some crushed ice.

- Look at photos of people or pets you care about.

- Draw a picture.

- Sing a lively song.

- Dance.

- Put some white craft glue on your hand, let it dry, and peel it off.

- Close your eyes and imagine yourself in a favorite place (real or imagined).

- Do something nice for someone else.

- Write a letter to someone you haven't seen in a long time.

- Take it out on a punching bag.

- Google "distracting activities" and find things to do.

- Listen to a favorite song or piece of music.

- Do something outside (garden, make a snow angel, rake leaves, shovel the driveway).

- Do a crossword, word search, Sudoku, or other kind of puzzle.

- Remind yourself of a time when things have been more difficult.

- Go somewhere to people-watch.

- Listen to babies laughing (IRL or online).

- Watch a movie.

Later in the chapter, you'll come up with a list of your own crisis survival skills, starting with the ones you do already and adding on others that appeal to you. Making a list of these activities and keeping it with you is really important; we all know how hard it is to think straight when emotions take over, and having a list takes the thinking out of the equation—you just pull out your list, and it tells you what to do.

Soothing Yourself

It's important to do things on a daily basis that are soothing for you. If you take good care of yourself on a regular basis, you will likely be more equipped to manage emotions that arise and will find that problems don't turn into crisis situations as often. In addition, of course, these skills are going to be helpful in a crisis. Again, there are probably things that you do already that are soothing, and you'll want to include these in your list of crisis survival skills.

Activity: How Can You Soothe Yourself?

For each of the senses, look at the examples provided and think about what might be soothing for you; add these to your list of crisis survival skills in the activity at the end of this section.

Sight: look at someone you care about (or pictures of them); watch nature scenes on the internet; look at your favorite painting; look at pictures of your favorite vacation.

Smell: put on your favorite lotion or perfume, or smell the scent of someone you love; smell a flower; go stand in a field or forest and breathe in the scents of nature.

Sound: listen to a favorite song (one that won't trigger you!) or listen to the sound of waves, thunder, or other nature sounds that you find soothing; if you can, get a recording of someone you care about saying soothing things to you, so you can listen to it when you can't talk to that person.

Taste: drink an herbal tea; suck on your favorite candy; occasionally treat yourself to your favorite meal or snack.

Touch: give someone a hug; pet your dog or cat; have a hot bath or shower; crawl under your favorite fuzzy or weighted blanket.

Alternate Rebellion

This skill sounds cool, doesn't it? The idea behind this DBT skill of *alternate rebellion* is that you're satisfying your urge to act out in a way that doesn't do harm to yourself or others (Linehan 1993). If you notice that your urge to do your target behavior is related to a desire to rebel—against your parents, or societal norms, or perhaps even pressure you've been putting on yourself to be successful, achieve, be perfect, and so on—you can turn to alternate rebellion (Linehan 2014).

Activity: How Can You Rebel in Nondamaging Ways?

Here are some ways that you could express your desire to rebel without the negative consequences of your target behavior. Check off any you would be willing to try, and add your own ideas in the space provided at the end of this list.

☐ Dye your hair a crazy color.

☐ Wear crazy underwear.

☐ Wear mismatched socks or shoes (or both).

☐ Say no to someone's reasonable request, and don't give them an explanation.

☐ Turn your music up loud.

☐ Go into your basement and scream as loud as you can.

☐ Throw your pillow (or something else that's soft) at the wall.

☐ Kiss your dog on the lips.

☐ Put your pants on starting with the opposite leg.

☐ Get a piercing or tattoo.

☐ Express a viewpoint different to what's considered the norm.

☐ Give an honest response instead of a polite one.

☐ Start a food fight.

Add your own ideas here:

_____

_____

Of course, it's always important to respect others and ourselves, so keep in mind that context is important. Starting a food fight in the school cafeteria or in the fancy restaurant where your parents took you for your birthday? Probably not a good idea. Turning your music up loud when your parent is in the house trying to sleep? Not likely to win you any brownie points. But hopefully, you can find some activities that will help you not act on those urges to engage in your target behaviors.

Activity: Your List of Crisis Survival Skills

Go back and review the earlier examples of distracting and self-soothing skills and non-damaging ways of rebelling, and using these and your own ideas, create your own list of crisis survival skills. It's important that you personalize these skills to fit you. Challenge yourself to make your list as long as possible.

_____

_____

_____

_____

_____

_____

_____

_____

_____

_____

Because you never know when a crisis might strike, it's a good idea to have this list with you at all times, so make a couple of copies and think about where you may want to keep them. You'll want easy access to these ideas when you need a reminder of what to do when your emotions start to get more intense. You can also take a picture to keep on your phone or tablet.

Other Skills to Get You Through the Crisis

Remember the goal with these skills is to help you not do the target behaviors that are going to make things worse for you, and what's helpful will be different for everyone. Look at the suggestions below and see what other skills you can add to your crisis survival list that will increase your chances of getting through the crisis.

Do a Relaxation Exercise

Many types of relaxation exercises can be helpful. Progressive muscle relaxation (PMR) can be especially useful in a crisis, because when emotions start to arise, you probably tense your muscles. The more tense you feel, the more stressed out you will get. Letting go of that tension can be a simple (though not easy!) way to let go of stress or at least keep your emotions from becoming even more intense. With PMR, you focus on tensing and then releasing each muscle group, starting with your feet and slowly moving upward until you get to your head (or if you prefer, you can go in the opposite direction, from head to feet). Here are some instructions to do either lying down or seated in a chair:

1. Feet: Curl your toes downward, and tense your feet. Now let go.

2. Lower legs and feet: Flex your feet, pulling your toes toward you. Release them.

3. Legs: Squeeze your thigh muscles while doing the first two steps again. Release.

4. Hands: Clench your fists.

5. Arms: Keeping your fists clenched, bring your forearms up toward your shoulders, like you're showing off your biceps! Lower and relax. Unclench your fists.

6. Buttocks: Squeeze them tight! Then release.

7. Stomach: Suck in those abs! Then release them.

8. Chest: Take a deep breath. Then release it.

9. Neck and shoulders: Raise your shoulders up to your ears. Then release.

10. Mouth: Open your mouth as wide as it can go! Close it and relax.

11. Eyes: Squeeze your eyelids shut. Then release the tension.

12. Forehead: Raise your eyebrows as high as they'll go. Now lower them and relax.

While you're doing this, be careful not to squeeze your muscles so hard that you hurt yourself; the idea here is to relax your muscles, not to find another way of self-harming! There are lots of online tutorials that can walk you through PMR, and you might want to do this with instruction until you get the hang of it. Over time, you'll find you can also take shortcuts, tensing and releasing several muscle groups at the same time. Give PMR a try and find your groove. Of course, there are also many other ways of practicing relaxation, so if you don't like this one, try another, such as body scan or guided imagery.

Whatever relaxation exercise you decide to use, it's best if you practice when you're feeling calm, to get comfortable and familiar with the exercise so that you'll know how to use it in a crisis. Once you're comfortable with it, add it to your list of crisis survival skills.

Create a Calm Place

Some people like to have a calm, peaceful, soothing, or secure place they create in their imagination to help them cope in times of stress. This calm place could be based on a real place, or it could be completely made up. Here are some examples to get you thinking of what your calm place might look like:

A sandy, private beach (maybe your favorite vacation spot?)

A room in your house that's comfortable (with a lock on the door?)

A rock by a lake or stream

The mountains

Again, it's important to find what works best for you. When you have time, find a comfortable spot where you won't be disturbed, and then take some time to imagine your calm place. Create this place with as much detail as possible, and practice going there in your mind. Like any skill, going to your calm place will be easier in times of distress if you've practiced doing this when things were going fairly smoothly. If going to a calm place appeals to you, put it on your list of crisis survival skills.

Prayer

For some people, prayer can be helpful when things get really difficult. You don't have to be religious to pray; you might pray to your god, or you might pray to a higher power, or to your own internal wisdom or even to the universe. If you like, add this to your list of crisis survival skills to remind yourself to use it.

Write a Letter to Yourself

Often people can get to a state of mind where they know what's healthy for them and what will help them work toward their long-term goals. When you have a period of wisdom or clearheadedness like this, write yourself a letter reminding you of why you want to live a healthier life without these problem behaviors. Remind yourself of the goals you're working toward. Maybe you can recall a time in your life when things were better and you didn't use the target behavior; if so, you can write about what that was like and why you want to get back there. Reading this letter to yourself can be very helpful when things get distressing, so this needs to go on your crisis survival list as well.

Safety Box

It can also be helpful to have a safety box handy, where you keep things that will help you to not act on urges. Here are some examples of what might go in your safety box:

Your letter to yourself

Body lotion

Candy or gum

Stress ball

Bubbles

Your favorite book

Dried flowers

Inspirational messages

A souvenir from a favorite trip

Slinky

Playdough

Photographs

Fidget toy

Coloring book

Things from your family and friends that remind you you're loved

Whatever you decide to put in your safety box, make what you put in soothing; distracting; reminders of why you don't want to act on this urge; reminders of your long-term goals and pleasurable memories; and so on. And don't forget to put your safety box on your list of crisis survival skills!

Steps to Managing Your Urge

Now it's time to put all of these skills together to help you not act on the urge to self-harm or self-destruct.

Step 1: When you notice the urge, rate it on a scale of 1 (it's there, but barely noticeable) to 10 (it's super intense).

Step 2: Pull out your phone or tablet, go to your alarm clock, or go to the kitchen and use the timer on the stove, and set an alarm for fifteen minutes. Promise yourself that for the next fifteen minutes you're going to use skills instead of acting on the urge.

Step 3: Go back to the pros and cons chart you filled out in chapter 1, and remind yourself of all of the reasons why you don't want to act on the urge. Better yet, review your chart before you get into a crisis, and make a separate list of all the cons of engaging in the behavior along with all the pros of not engaging in it, so you've got this list handy to review when the urge comes up. You can either keep this list in your safety box or—you guessed it—add it to your list of crisis survival skills!

Step 4: Pull out your list of crisis survival skills, and do the first thing on the list. If it's "call Josie" (your best friend), but it's midnight and you know she's fast asleep, then go on to the next thing. If it's "go for a walk," but it's midnight and not safe for you to walk alone, go on to the next thing. This is why you want your list to be as long as possible. You might also find that when you try to "watch TV," you're not able to concentrate on your show, because you're too emotional, so—you got it—go on to the next thing. Keep doing this until your timer goes off. Some survival skills are going to be more effective at certain times than others, but the key is to keep using the skills until your timer goes off. Remember, you want to delay acting on the urge, to get you through the crisis without making it worse.

Step 5: When your timer goes off after fifteen minutes, rate your urge again. If it's lower, then hopefully you can pat yourself on the back for a job well done and continue with your day. If the urge has stayed the same or maybe even increased, then ideally you want to set the timer for another fifteen minutes and return to using your skills. Even if you don't—if instead you give in and do the thing you're trying not to do—you still need to congratulate yourself for using your skills first instead of going straight to that target behavior like you normally would have. This is progress. Gradually over time, you'll retrain yourself to use more and more skills as an alternative to immediately acting on the urge. It's hard work, it takes lots of practice, and, as you hopefully already know, it will be worth it in the long run.

Wrapping Up

This chapter introduced the skills that are going to keep you from making things worse for yourself. If you've begun using them already, you are off to a great start. Remember that the skills you've been learning so far aren't going to take away your pain or solve your problems, so do your best not to get frustrated if things don't seem to be changing that much. The next chapter will introduce one of the skills that will help you solve your problems and do things differently in the long run. This skill is called mindfulness. So, hang in there, make sure you're using the skills you've learned as best as you can, and when you're ready...turn the page.

Chapter 3

How to Get Your Groove On

Right now, I'm sitting at my computer, the sun is shining in through the window, I'm feeling tired, and I'm having the thought, *It's Saturday, and I really don't feel like working.* I'm noticing the urge to stop working and to do something fun instead. But because I'm being mindful right now, I'm just noticing the urge to stop working. I'm not automatically acting on it; and I'm choosing to continue to work, because I know it's in my best interest in the long run. (It's February, so it's pretty cold outside, and the more work I do now, the more I'll be able to enjoy the weather when it warms up in May!)

This is one way that mindfulness can be helpful when it comes to target behaviors: you can notice a thought, feeling, physical sensation, or urge, and not have to do anything about it. You can *choose* how you'd like to act rather than just react to your experience. The next exercise will help you look at some other possible benefits of bringing this skill into your life.

Activity: Why Practice Mindfulness?

Put a check mark beside the behaviors you know you engage in, even some of the time.

Dwelling, rehashing, or ruminating

☐ Thinking about things that happened in the past (whether it's yesterday, last month, last year, or ten years ago)

☐ Reliving or replaying events of the past in your head or imagining different outcomes for situations that are already over

☐ Feeling sadness, regret, guilt, shame, anger, and other painful emotions about things in the past

☐ Creating imaginary scenarios in your head about things that haven't happened yet

☐ Noticing the words "what if" coming to your mind

Concentration and memory

☐ Struggling to focus on one thing at a time

☐ Losing your train of thought during conversation with others or while doing activities like watching television or reading

☐ Forgetting things that have happened recently or missing important deadlines or appointments

☐ Zoning out or acting on automatic pilot when doing a task

☐ Misplacing or losing things

Missing out on pleasurable emotions

☐ Missing out on pleasurable moments because you're so focused on the negative

☐ Dividing your attention between what you're doing in the present and what you did in the past or might do in the future

☐ Not stopping to smell the roses

☐ Being negative or judgmental

Trouble relaxing

☐ Having problems sleeping

☐ Having racing thoughts

☐ Feeling overwhelmed with everything you have to do much of the time

☐ Focusing on more than one thing at a time

☐ Feeling fearful, anxious, or nervous

Getting to Know Yourself

☐ Not having a good sense of who you are as a person

☐ Not being aware of your values, what's important to you

☐ Being passive and letting others make decisions for you most of the time

☐ Following the leader instead of figuring things out for yourself

☐ Having a strong need to fit in

Mindfulness can help in all of these areas. It can help you get your groove on, by helping you be in the present moment more often, reducing emotional pain, improving concentration and memory, increasing pleasurable emotions, and improving your ability to relax. It can help you get to know who you are and work toward who you would like to be. Take a look at the following story that demonstrates some of these ideas.

Oliver's Story

Oliver had been struggling with feelings of depression and anxiety, and he had been turning to burning or punching himself at times. Part of this was to help him refocus and get his mind off the emotional pain he was feeling, but part of it was because he felt so ashamed and angry at himself for being "weak" that he felt he deserved it. He had also been stealing things because he found the rush of this helped him feel better in the short term, but this just increased his feelings of guilt and shame, and it turned into one messed-up cycle.

Oliver's parents pushed him to get involved in a robotics club at school. He didn't really want to, but he liked robotics and it got his parents off his back, so he went anyway. At the encouragement of his therapist, he had been practicing mindfulness for short periods while he was there. One day at the club after school, his cell phone went off, and he realized it was a reminder to take his medication before dinner. He couldn't believe how caught up he'd been in that moment, just in the zone, fully engaged and participating in what he was doing. He also realized that for a full two hours, he hadn't once felt depressed, anxious, ashamed, or angry, and he hadn't had any urges to hurt himself.

Have you ever had this experience? Where you're just in the groove, going with the flow, in the zone? Most of us have gotten there at times without trying. Mindfulness can help us get there more often and spend more time there.

What Is Mindfulness?

Mindfulness is when you're doing one thing at a time in the present moment, with your full attention, and with acceptance. For Oliver, when he was working on his project in the robotics club, mindfulness meant focusing on just that: interacting with his partner as they worked on their project together, accepting problems as they arose, and thinking about how to solve them and so on. When you're doing your homework mindfully, you're just doing your homework; if you're rehearsing lines for the school play mindfully, you're only rehearsing; if you're playing Monopoly with your brother, that's all you're doing. Of course, your thoughts will wander as you do that activity, but mindfulness means that you just notice when your thoughts wander and practice *acceptance* (you do your best to not judge yourself for wandering onto whatever is distracting you from the moment, or for whatever thoughts or feelings might arise); whatever is happening, you do your best to just notice, and you bring your attention back to the present. This is mindfulness.

The opposite of mindfulness is mind*less*ness, or being on automatic pilot: doing things while not fully present and paying attention. You allow yourself to get caught up in your usual thoughts, so you are not in the present; you are probably judgmental, jumping to conclusions and making assumptions, and so on. The following activity will give you a better understanding of what mindfulness is (and isn't).

Activity: Is It Mindfulness or Mindlessness?

In each of the following situations, identify whether the person was being *mindful* or *mindless*.

1. Tamara was feeling very sad and to help her get through this current crisis, she decided to walk her dog. As they walked, she noticed her thoughts continuously

going back to the fight she had had with her girlfriend, but she would notice these thoughts, and as best as she could, she would refocus her attention on the walk. She paid attention to Charlie sniffing at everything, noticed the feel of the sun on her face, looked at the trees they passed and the kids playing in the park. She did her best to not judge herself as her thoughts were wandering a lot and she was still feeling very hurt and angry.

Was this an example of being mindful or mindless? _____

2. Carson was worried about not making the basketball team this year. When tryouts came, he looked at everyone else, and he realized that so many of the other guys were way better than he was. He realized also that he hadn't practiced nearly as much as he should have, and it showed in how lousy his game was now. He was also a lot shorter than many of the players, and he couldn't help thinking to himself that there was no way he was going to make the team.

Was this an example of being mindful or mindless? _____

3. Jamal and his best friend had had a huge fight the day before, and Jamal was struggling with feeling angry and hurt, and he was having urges to cut to help him deal with those feelings. He knew the fact that he hadn't slept the night before was making things more difficult, and he did his best to just notice how he was feeling; he noticed the judgmental thoughts about Carson coming up—*He's a bad friend, he shouldn't have treated me that way*, and so on—and he did his best to just notice these thoughts and let them go. He didn't want to act on the urge to hurt himself, so he pulled out his list of crisis survival skills and did his best to get his mind off the situation.

Was this an example of being mindful or mindless? _____

4. Katie had been dealing with anger problems for a long time. She had recently found that breathing deeply, focusing on just her breath, in the morning helped her prevent emotional distress during the day. She was getting into the habit of doing this breathing every day before she got out of bed. She would notice when her attention wandered and bring her full attention back to her breathing, and she would do her best to not judge whatever she noticed in that moment, either

within herself (like her thoughts about how "stupid" this was or her feelings of anger when she noticed them there) or in her environment (like her sister blaring her music this early in the morning in the next room).

Was this an example of being mindful or mindless? _____

Tamara, Jamal, and Katie all practiced mindfulness, each in their own way.

You can practice mindfulness in a lot of different ways—actually, in an infinite number of ways! In fact, whatever you're doing, you can bring mindfulness to it. For instance, you could choose to read this paragraph mindfully: you would intentionally bring your full attention to *just reading*; you notice when your attention wanders, and without judging yourself for wandering (for having an emotion or a specific thought come up or for whatever distracted you), you bring your attention back to reading. Or, like Katie, you can choose to do a specific mindfulness practice: you could breathe mindfully, do a body scan mindfully, or listen to guided imagery—there are lots of apps for that! It really doesn't matter how you practice, as long as you practice. Whatever you choose to do, it's important to be patient with yourself and to understand that, as with any useful skill, mindfulness will take time and effort to learn and to get better at, but it will be worth it in the long run.

Mindfulness can help you notice the good in life. When struggling with emotions, whether it's with sadness, anxiety, anger, shame, or other pain, it can be hard to notice when opportunities for small pleasant emotions do arise. This is another way that mindfulness helps. Try the following activity to practice using mindfulness.

Activity: Increasing Pleasurable Emotions with Mindfulness

Think of something that you like to do; something you do for yourself, because it's enjoyable, calming, peaceful, relaxing, interesting, soothing, or because it generates some other kind of pleasurable emotion. It could be reading a book, playing with your pet, rehearsing your lines for the school play, going for a walk by the lake, or something else.

Choose an activity, find a comfortable place where you won't be disturbed, and then do the activity mindfully for a couple of minutes or so, following these steps:

1. Write down the activity here. _____

2. Begin to do your activity.

3. Notice when your attention wanders.

4. Gently, without judging yourself or anything or anyone else, bring your attention back to the activity.

5. Notice any pleasurable feelings you have while doing the activity, such as peace or contentment, satisfaction, or maybe even enjoyment.

6. Repeat steps 3 and 4 as needed (you may need to do this over and over again).

7. When you are ready, end the activity.

Here's another tip for how to notice and enjoy those pleasurable emotions more. If you notice any worry thoughts—about when the pleasurable feelings will end or whether you deserve to feel pleasure, or about anything else—do not judge the thoughts or yourself for having them or the feelings they might trigger, but just bring yourself back to the activity and pleasurable feelings.

So, what was this like? What did you notice? Were you able to accept what you noticed, to allow it to be without trying to change it? This can be hard, especially when your experience is something you don't like. But this is how you learn that you can have something uncomfortable happen (whether it's an itchy foot or a feeling of sadness), and you can tolerate it, and it will actually change. Yes, sometimes the experience gets more intense, but often it gets more bearable, and sometimes something else comes up to distract you from it.

What Are You Practicing?

It's probably not news to you that what you practice, you get better at. That's why you practice running track, or swimming, or playing the drums, or doing math. But the same holds true for how we think. For example, when you think about the past over and over again, maybe replaying in your head an argument you had with your parents when you lost it and yelled and screamed, what you're getting better at is thinking about the past and losing your temper. Likewise, when you're letting your mind go to worry thoughts about the future or getting caught up in judgmental thoughts about yourself or others, these are the habits you're strengthening. So mindfulness also helps in this way: when you become aware that you're falling back into an old thought or behavior habit, it gives you the opportunity to stop that particular thought or behavior and practice something else mindfully, which can then start to become a stronger thought or behavior than the old one.

Activity: Recognizing Your Habits

Look at the list and check off the thoughts and behaviors that you've been practicing. If you can think of any others, add them at the end.

☐ Rehashing the past

☐ Worrying about the future

☐ Trying to suppress or stuff thoughts and feelings

☐ Researching self-harm or suicide

☐ Fantasizing about doing self-harm or self-destructive behaviors

☐ Reliving past episodes of your target behavior

☐ Judging yourself or others

☐ Other habits you practice:

_____

_____

The first step in changing any behavior (including thinking patterns) is to become aware of it. Now that you're learning a bit more about the things you've been doing and thinking that are problems, and that are likely contributing to your target behavior, you'll be better able to use new skills to change these things.

Getting to Know Yourself

As a teen, you're still figuring out who you are—what's important to you, what you like, believe in, and want out of life. This is what you're supposed to be doing, but it can be hard to do when you're a highly sensitive person growing up in an invalidating environment. Many people learn to invalidate themselves—they learn that they shouldn't be feeling what they feel, or thinking what they think, and they get very good at pushing away their own thoughts and emotions, trying to figure out from others what they *should* be thinking or feeling instead. Does this sound familiar? Are you a more passive person, going along with the crowd because you're afraid to rock the boat? When out with friends, are you the one who says, "Let's go see the latest Marvel movie," or do you say, "It doesn't matter to me, what do you want to see?" when it actually does matter to you and you do have a preference?

Okay, so you might be wondering what on earth this has to do with self-harm and self-destructive behaviors. Knowing yourself better, including who you want to be as a person, will help you recognize that keeping these behaviors in your life isn't helping you move toward your long-term goals. It's also true that being passive much of the time leads to more emotional pain, as you often aren't getting your needs met. Getting to know yourself better will make it easier to express your needs, and this will in turn reduce those urges to do target behaviors. I'm guessing that if these target behaviors were okay for you, you wouldn't still be reading this book. So it's time to take a closer look at what's most important to you.

Activity: What Are Your Values?

Think about your beliefs, what's most important to, or what matters most to you, such as being successful, loyal, or physically and emotionally healthy. You might already have a sense of what some of your values are. If so, list them here:

_____

_____

_____

_____

_____

If you don't already know what your values are, no worries. Think of someone you look up to. It could be someone close to you, a family member or friend; it could be a teacher, coach, or guidance counselor; or it could be someone you've never met, like a political or public figure or a famous person. What is it about this person that you admire? What do you like about them? What do you see in this person that you would like to be?

_____

_____

If you're still coming up blank, here is a list of things that people often identify as important to them. Check off those that you would say are important to you:

- ☐ Having healthy relationships

- ☐ Being responsible

- ☐ Being healthy

- ☐ Learning

- ☐ Focusing on family

- ☐ Achieving things in life (working hard, getting good grades, being financially secure)

- ☐ Having good character (integrity, honesty, standing up for your beliefs, being respectful)

- ☐ Contributing (volunteering your time, giving back to your community, being generous)

- ☐ Enjoying life

- ☐ Stewardship (such as taking care of the environment)

☐ Being part of a group or community

☐ Advocating for equality

Now think about the values you've identified, and think about the person you would like to be. Envision yourself living a life worth living (Linehan 1993), where perhaps you have a career, or a family, or you're surrounding yourself with people you care about, or you're doing other things that are meaningful to you in some way. Do your target behaviors fit into that life?

Hopefully the answer to that question is no. Here's another opportunity for you to remind your self-harming or self-destructive side that this isn't a behavior you want to continue. You might make a photocopy of your values and put it somewhere you'll see it as a reminder of these things that are important to you, or draw a picture or make a collage that represents this life you'd like for yourself, and hang it on your wall. If you started this in chapter 2, you can add to the image you've already made. Reminders are important because they can help you get to your internal wisdom—yes, you do have it, more on that soon!—when you start to experience urges to do unhealthy things.

Wrapping Up

Hopefully, you're starting to see some of the many ways that mindfulness is going to help you. As with all the skills in this book, the key is to practice it. It's important to understand your reasons for practicing. Equally important, though, is finding ways to practice that work for you, so do some experimenting with different ways of practicing mindfulness, remembering that you can truly do anything mindfully.

Many of the other skills you'll be looking at shortly will deepen your understanding of mindfulness. The next chapter will continue to help you learn new ways of not acting on those urges—and instead get to your own internal wisdom more often—so you'll be one step closer to living your values and eliminating those target behaviors.

Chapter 4

Finding Your Internal Wisdom

Most people have times when they become so emotional that their thinking shuts down. For some people, the opposite happens: it's easier to turn off the emotions and focus just on the reasoning, pushing away emotions and avoiding the pain. Either option can be okay in the short term, if it's not something that happens regularly, but in the long run, this out-of-balance state can get people into trouble and cause more problems. In the long run, you want to be able to get to a healthier, more balanced middle ground between your emotions and your reasoning. In this chapter, you'll learn about three different thinking styles that we all have and how to get to a more balanced place, so you can make healthier, wiser choices.

Three Different Perspectives

Most people can relate to having three different ways of thinking about things, or three different perspectives: our reasoning self, our emotional self, and our wise self (Linehan 1993). Keep in mind that everyone has all three, but many people notice they spend more time in one than the others. As you learn more about these thinking styles, think about your own experience and whether you tend to act more from one perspective than others.

The Reasoning Self

Your *reasoning self* is the part of you that you access when you're thinking logically, using straightforward, factual, matter-of-fact thinking. You're doing your math homework, for example, writing out study notes for exams, or figuring out how much money you need to save to buy yourself the latest piece of technology. When you're in your reasoning self, there's typically no emotion involved, but if there is, it's on the back burner, and it's not influencing your behavior (this could be because there isn't really an emotion to feel, or it could be because you're stuffing it, whether on purpose or not). People who spend a lot of time in this reasoning state tend to be described as "cold" or even "robotic." Think Spock or Data from *Star Trek*, or Sheldon from the *The Big Bang Theory*—these are perfect examples of people who are in their reasoning selves most (or all!) of the time.

Think of a recent time when you acted from your reasoning, thinking, logical, factual self, and write about it here:

_____

_____

The Emotional Self

Your *emotional self* is when your emotions take over and control you so that you're reacting from or being driven by them. If you're feeling hurt, angry, ashamed, or sad, for example, you might self-harm, or you might lash out at the person who hurt you. With anxiety, people often want to avoid the thing that's making them feel anxious. These are examples of an emotion controlling you. You may regret your behaviors later because they've made things worse for you. The Incredible Hulk and the Tasmanian Devil are great examples of someone being controlled by this emotional self. But it's important to know that your emotional self can also take over with pleasurable emotions and situations: for example, you win a scholarship for college, you feel super excited, and you call your family and friends to share your amazing news. Even if it's a pleasurable emotion that's controlling you, this is still your emotional self, and it can be problematic, like if you start dating someone new, and you're feeling love (or lust!) for that person. This is a pleasurable feeling, but it might drive you to make some unhealthy choices.

Think of a recent time when you acted from your emotional self (from a painful or pleasurable feeling), and write about it here:

_____

_____

The Wise Self

While you don't want to get rid of your emotional or reasoning selves (you need them both), it's good to be able to access your wise self. Your *wise self* is the middle ground between your reasoning and emotional selves. It's like the balanced place Yoda teaches his Jedi Knights about, where you're able to feel your feelings and you're still able to access your reasoning. You're able to combine these and use your internal wisdom—that sense of *knowing* that you've probably experienced before—to figure out what's in your best interest in the current situation.

Acting from your wise self, though, is also about acting from your values, and for most people, it's important to take others' perspectives into consideration. When a situation involves someone else you care about—whether it's your parents or siblings, your best friend, or your significant other—you typically consider not just your own thoughts, feelings, and desires but also those of the other person involved; this is how to keep relationships healthy. So you're going to consider others' perspectives when you're acting from your internal wisdom. Here are some examples of wise self:

- You have an urge to cut, and instead you set your timer and pull out your list of crisis survival skills.

- You feel lonely, and instead of starting a fight with your best friend to get him to pay attention to you, you reach out to him and tell him how you're feeling.

- You have an urge to not eat, as a punishment for the low mark you got on your chem test, but instead you force yourself to have some cheese and crackers.

Keep in mind that we all act from our wise self regularly although we may not notice it, because it often doesn't have the same negative consequences as acting from our thinking or feeling self. But when you push yourself to get up and go to school or to your part-time job even when you don't feel like it, that's usually your wise self. When your parents are getting on your case about cleaning your room *yet again,* and you pull out the vacuum, that's probably your inner wisdom telling you what to do.

Think of a recent time when you've acted from your wise self, using that internal sense of knowing, and write about it here:

_____

_____

Activity: Who's in Charge?

To help you get the hang of these three different perspectives, read the following story about Tess, and see if you can figure out which responses represent her reasoning, emotional, and wise self:

Tess always wanted to be a veterinarian. As a high school junior, she met with her guidance counselor, who told her it was unlikely she'd be able to accomplish this goal because Tess had always struggled in the sciences.

1. Tess left the guidance counselor's office feeling disheartened and disappointed. She went home and, after binge-eating to help her cope with her emotions, she started working on resigning herself to the fact that she would never reach her goal of being a vet. Which self was in control?

    Reasoning Self   Emotional Self   Wise Self

2. Tess left the guidance counselor's office choosing to ignore the feelings of disappointment that were coming up for her. Obviously, she wouldn't be able to be a vet (since the guidance counselor had said so, it must be true); she'd have to consider another career at some point, but as she didn't have to apply to college

for another year, she decided she just wouldn't think about it right now. Which self was in control?

Reasoning Self   Emotional Self   Wise Self

3. Tess left the guidance counselor's office feeling disappointed and hurt that the guidance counselor was discouraging her from pursuing her dream. She knew her science marks hadn't been great, and she knew it would take a lot of hard work, but she thought this dream was worth pursuing. She would talk to her parents about the possibility of a tutor and see if she could get her grades up in her final years of high school. If that didn't work, then she acknowledged that she'd have to have a backup plan, but she wasn't ready to quit just yet. Which self was in control?

Reasoning Self   Emotional Self   Wise Self

Tess's emotional self was in charge when she gave up on her ambition, in reaction to what the counselor had told her, and coped with her feelings by bingeing. Her reasoning self was in control when she gave up and ignored her feelings of disappointment. Listening to her wise self, however, she was motivated not to give up without trying harder to accomplish her goal. Hopefully, you're starting to get a better understanding of these three perspectives. The idea is not that you're always acting from your wise self but that you have awareness of what is driving your behavior and have the option of moving toward that more balanced wise self when you want or need to.

Activity: What Does Your Reasoning, Emotional, and Wise Self Say?

In this activity you're going to be thinking about what each of these perspectives looks like for you. The goal here is to make sure you have a way of really relating to each of these thinking styles so that your wise self will be more accessible.

1. Start by choosing a recent difficult situation you experienced. This could be anything, like having a fight with someone, an urge to do a target behavior, or your

friends canceling plans on you. Sticking to the facts as best as you can, write a description of that situation here:

_____

_____

2. Thinking back on this situation, jot some notes about what your reasoning perspective was. Alternatively, if you had no reasoning perspective at the time, how do you think about it from a logical, reasoning place now?

_____

_____

3. Next, write about your emotional perspective. Were you acting from your emotions in some way or at least having strong urges? What emotion-related thoughts did you notice? For example, were you judging yourself or others?

_____

_____

4. And finally, write some notes about what you know, from your inner wisdom, about this situation. You might not have had this wise perspective in the middle of the situation; if that was the case, write about what your wise self tells you now:

_____

_____

Many of the skills in this book will help you get to your wise self (such as the skill of mindfulness that you learned in chapter 3). But when you're trying to change something, the best place to start is usually to pay attention to it and have more awareness of when that behavior is happening. Moving forward, do your best to check in with yourself throughout the day, just to see what thinking perspective you're in—your reasoning, your emotional, or your wise self.

Changing a behavior is usually difficult, and it can often help if you write down your intention. Take a moment to consider what you're going to start doing to help you remember to check in to see what state of mind you're in. Examples might be putting a daily recurring appointment in your cell phone to remind you to ask yourself what state of mind you're in; putting a sticky note on your laptop or somewhere else you will see it every day; or every time you do a particular activity like pouring yourself a glass of water, you'll ask yourself what state of mind you're in at that moment. Once you've decided on a strategy, write it down here:

_____

_____

It can also help to have different people in mind who represent these different perspectives for you. Then, in a difficult situation, you can bring to mind these people as a shortcut to help you figure out what perspective you're thinking from and then get to a more balanced perspective. For example, you could ask yourself, *What would Mom do?* if your mother represents a wise self perspective.

Activity: Your Wise Person Shortcut

Think of three people to represent your three different perspectives. They could be people you don't know, like actors, sports stars, political or religious figures, or historical or even fictional characters. Or you can think of people in your life who represent these perspectives, like one of your parents or another relative, a best friend, coach, or teacher. You can use examples from this chapter if you like, but the main thing is that the people you choose make sense for you. Who represents a reasoning self, an emotional self, and a wise self for you?

Reasoning person: _____

Emotional person: _____

Wise person: _____

Now when you need to find some internal wisdom, you can ask, *What would my wise person say?*

Getting to Your Wise Self

As with any new skill, getting to your wise self can be difficult to do at the best of times, never mind when your emotions get really intense and your thinking shuts down, or your thinking takes over and you fall back into old avoidance behaviors. To get better at getting to your wise self, you need to practice. Here are some ideas to help. I suggest trying them all, starting with the one that fits best for you and practicing it as often as you can until getting to your wise self comes more naturally.

- Ask yourself a question, such as *What does my inner wisdom tell me?* or *What would my wise person do or tell me in this situation?* Then listen quietly for an answer. You might want to close your eyes to do this.

- Practice breathing to get to that wise state of mind: you might pair some paced breathing (see chapter 2) with a saying of some sort, such as "Get to…" (on the inhale) "my wise self" (on the exhale). Make this fit for you.

- If you like images, you might visualize yourself turning inward to get to your internal wisdom. Many people feel their wise place inside themselves, sometimes near their heart, sometimes further down in the area of deep breathing. You might get a picture of your own wise, knowing place in your head and imagine yourself going there.

Remember, your practice should feel comfortable, so experiment with these and others that you might make up yourself. If this is hard for you at the beginning, and you're not sure if you're getting to your wise place, you may want to ask someone you trust (like your wise person) if they think you're acting from your reasoning, emotional, or wise self. This can help you learn what each of these perspectives feels like, until you get more confident and can rely on yourself to figure it out. The next step is to work on ways to reduce the amount of time that you get stuck in your emotional self.

Reducing the Emotional Hijack

Certain things you do may increase the likelihood of being taken over by your emotional self. This includes not getting enough sleep (or sleeping too much), not eating enough (or eating too much), and using substances. To keep from being hijacked by your emotional self, you can use the STRONG acronym to concentrate on how to reduce the likelihood of this happening:

Sleep. Not getting enough sleep or getting too much sleep makes it more likely that you'll be controlled by your emotions. Adults need seven to nine hours of sleep a night, and young people need more, usually between eight and eleven hours, depending on your age. The best way to figure out how much sleep you need is to consciously think about how tired or energetic you feel every day and how well your brain is functioning—can you think straight, concentrate, and remember things? The bottom line here is that, if you're not getting the right amount of sleep, you're more likely to be taken over by your emotional self, putting you at risk for those target behaviors.

Treat health problems, both physical and emotional. This means taking medications as prescribed by your doctor and following other treatment recommendations. This might include seeing your psychotherapist or attending a group to help you manage emotions or attending your physiotherapy appointments if you have an injury or a chronic pain condition. Physical health conditions can contribute to emotional problems, so whether it's something chronic like diabetes, an injury causing ongoing pain, or something shorter term like having a cold, taking care of your body is also a way to take care of your mind. Most of us are more emotional (grumpy!) when we're not feeling well.

Resist using substances. Drugs and alcohol are referred to as *mood-altering substances* because they alter our mood, and we have no way of controlling this. Using substances can be a self-destructive behavior, and even if you're not abusing them, it's still important for you to consider whether substance use is something you need to resist. Drugs and alcohol put you at risk of being controlled by your emotions, and when you're already struggling in this way, not using can be another way of tackling the problem. You may find that you're more emotionally sensitive for days after using—not just at the time of use and during the hangover or crash that comes the next day—so it's important for you to be aware of how substances affect you in the longer term.

One thing a day to build mastery. Doing something every day that gives you a sense of being in control of your world helps reduce the likelihood that your emotional self will take over. This means doing something that gives you a sense of pride in yourself for what you've accomplished. It might be an activity that you don't enjoy doing but feel good about after completing. For example, you might not like going to the gym to work out, but you feel good about yourself afterward, or you might hate doing homework, but once it's done, you enjoy the feeling of accomplishment. This builds your self-respect over time as well.

Nutrition. If you're not eating properly, your body will miss out on the nutrients it needs to do basic functions like breathing, blinking, and standing upright, never mind more complex things like thinking, concentrating, and remembering things. You may be eating too much, by regularly overeating or bingeing; not eating enough, by skipping meals or restricting calories; or not eating nutritious foods often enough. Eating in any of these ways will also make it more likely that you'll be ruled by your emotional self. It's also important to remember that some foods and beverages contain caffeine, which as a stimulant can contribute to feelings of anxiety, irritability, and poor sleep. Sugar is another substance that can increase emotional instability. By adjusting what you're putting into your body, you may be able to reduce the likelihood that you will be hijacked by your emotions.

Getting exercise. Some studies have shown that exercise that gets your heart rate up—cardiovascular exercise, like jogging or walking fast, dancing, or playing sports—is just as good at reducing depression as medication. Even if you don't have depression, exercise is obviously something that can improve your mood and help you manage your emotions in healthier ways.

You may find that you need to work on one or more of these areas in your life. This next exercise is followed by a worksheet where you can keep track of how well you're doing in each of these STRONG areas.

Activity: Getting STRONG

Decide which of the STRONG areas you want to work on to reduce your emotional reactions.

1. Which area do you want to work on first? You might want to work on more than one area, which is great, but pick one to start with:

   _____

2. What's your end goal in working on this area? For example, if you're working on sleeping better, do you need to increase or reduce your sleep? Do you know what your ideal number of hours is? If so, your goal might be "to get eight to nine hours of sleep each night." Or, if you're working on improving your eating, you might set a goal of "eating three meals and two snacks each day." Write your goal here:

   _____

3. Now think about the smaller steps that will get you moving in the direction of your end goal. (For example, if your goal is to get eight to nine hours of sleep each night, your first step might be to turn off your computer and any other devices an hour before bedtime, your next step might be going to bed fifteen minutes earlier than you usually do, and so on. If you tend to lie awake at night, you could make it a goal to start practicing a mindfulness exercise like those in chapter 3 or a relaxation exercise like progressive muscle relaxation, which you learned in chapter 2.) What steps will you take toward your goal?

   Step 1: _____

   Step 2: _____

   Step 3: _____

Begin with taking the first step. Then work on each step until you have accomplished your goal. If you have more than one STRONG goal, start with the first one and come back to the others later. Taking on too much at once will make it harder to reach your goals. Slow and steady is better.

Worksheet: STRONG Log

Here is a worksheet to help you keep track of changes you're making and the effects they might be having on your mood and functioning. The instructions follow.

STRONG Goal: _____

Date:	Monday	Tuesday	Wednesday	Thursday	Friday	Saturday	Sunday
Sadness/depression							
Anxiety							
Anger/irritability							
Guilt							
Shame							
Mood swings							
Energy							
Concentration							
Memory							

Start by filling in the STRONG goal that you're working on (such as "increase eating from one to two meals daily"; "increase sleep from seven to seven and a half hours"; "reduce use of alcohol to maximum of four drinks on Friday and Saturday only"). Fill in the date at the top of the chart, so you can begin to keep track of your progress (this will be useful later when you want to go back and review the changes you've made and the results). For the following week, pay attention to your emotions, mood swings, energy, concentration, and memory so you can report on these things at the end of each day. Begin by rating the degree to which you felt any of the emotions listed in the worksheet; choose a number on a scale from 0 (*that emotion wasn't present at all today*) to 5 (*that emotion was the highest it gets*). On the same scale, rate whether you had mood swings (where 0 was *not at all*, and 5 was *extreme swings*), how high your energy was (0 is *nonexistent*, and 5 is *high*), and concentration and memory (0 is *nonexistent*, and 5 is *really great*). If you want to keep track of other things that aren't on the worksheet, you can add them to the list.

After you've reached a goal and remained consistent with it for at least a couple of weeks, you might go on to your next goal. Start with a new worksheet every week. Visit http://www.newharbinger.com/45458 to download copies.

Wrapping Up

In this chapter, you've learned about the three different perspectives we all have, and you have begun working on getting to a place of inner wisdom. You've also learned about some of the things you may do that make you more likely to be controlled by your emotional self, and you've hopefully begun working on some goals to reduce this likelihood. Practicing these skills is super important, but don't rush yourself. Make sure you move at a pace that's comfortable for you.

In the next chapter, you'll get to know your emotions better, including naming them accurately. This will prepare you to learn other skills to better manage your emotions in the long run. In the meantime, make sure you continue to use the skills you've already learned. Keep up the fantastic work!

Chapter 5

Name the Feeling to Tame It

Many people have a hard time figuring out exactly what they're feeling when they're experiencing painful emotions. Do you find yourself often thinking that you feel upset or bad but are unable to put your finger on what emotion you're feeling? Although not uncommon, this is problematic in part because it's hard to figure out what you can do to help yourself with a feeling if you don't know what the feeling is—if you can't name it, you can't tame it. Because accurately naming your emotions is such an important skill, this chapter will focus on some of the more difficult emotions to give you a better understanding of these feelings, so you can put a name to them when they come up.

Camillo's Story

Camillo thought of himself as an anxious person. He didn't really know why and thought maybe it was part of his "depression," but he was generally anxious and at times would also have panic attacks. These were the times that he would turn to burning himself if he could, because he found that, weirdly, it helped him feel calmer, and other strategies he had learned to help him deal with the anxiety usually didn't help that much.

Through a DBT skills group at his school, Camillo started learning more about his emotions and began to realize that what he had always labeled as "anxiety" wasn't actually just anxiety. He already knew that he didn't really like himself, and in the group, he learned that he felt shame quite often and that this was partly due to his self-judgments. These self-judgments triggered anger toward himself, which he had been mistaking for anxiety. His shame would also cause him to try to please others—since he didn't like himself, he found it hard to believe that others could like him and he'd do whatever he could to keep people in his life. Unfortunately, that often left him feeling "used," because his friends came to count on him for rides and no one ever offered him money for gas (of course, if they had offered, Camillo wouldn't have taken it, because he wouldn't want them to get angry with him). Camillo realized that this was causing him to feel resentful. So, what he had always called "anxiety" was actually a combination of some anxiety (mostly a fear of being rejected by people), a lot of shame, and resentment. From this perspective, Camillo could think of all sorts of skills he could be using that would help with these emotions, and he could see why the strategies for anxiety weren't helping that much, since it was so much more than anxiety that he'd been dealing with all this time.

As you can see, emotions are pretty complicated! This chapter will help you untie your own complicated emotional knots. To begin, it will be helpful to take a closer look at what emotions are and what makes them so confusing.

What Is an Emotion?

Although we often call emotions "feelings," the feeling is just one part of the experience; emotions also involve our thoughts, body sensations, urges, and behaviors (Linehan 1993). Because there's so much going on when we're feeling an emotion, it can be easy to mix up emotions, thoughts, and behaviors. For example, if you're experiencing the emotion of anxiety, you're going to *feel* anxious in your body. Your *thought* might be *What if I can't do this?* And the *behavior* might be to avoid doing that thing. You might then end up saying "I feel like I can't do this," although this would be expressing a thought, not a feeling.

If you're experiencing the emotion of anger, you feel anger in your body. Your thought might be *This isn't fair.* And the behavior might be yelling at your parents. Again, you might confuse the feeling with the thought *I feel like this isn't fair.*

Putting a Name on It

There are a lot of different emotions, which is probably another reason we get confused about what we're feeling. This chapter will look at a few of the more painful emotions that often contribute to self-harming and self-destructive behaviors, but you can think of this as just a starting point. If you finish this chapter and still have questions about some of the emotions that cause problems for you—for some people, happiness, joy, love, and other pleasurable emotions can actually be problematic, for example—you'll need to do more work in this area.

The information in this chapter about anger, fear (often experienced as anxiety), sadness, guilt, and shame comes from Linehan (2014). All emotions serve a purpose or can be *justified* at times, which means that they make sense given the situation. Any of us can also feel emotions when they're *not* justified, and this can cause a lot of problems.

Anger

Anger's purpose. Anger is the emotion that usually comes up when there are obstacles in your path or when you or someone you care about is being attacked, threatened, insulted, or hurt by others. When a situation fits into one of these categories, you can say that the anger is justified; it makes sense given the situation.

What it does. Anger typically causes people to become aggressive; it might lead you to attack what you see as dangerous, to make the threat go away. When the human race was evolving, and there were constant threats in the environment, anger helped us survive.

Example of when anger is justified. Your parents ground you for breaking curfew; they are creating an obstacle that's getting in your way (you can't go to that party you were planning on). Therefore, it makes sense that you would feel angry in this situation; anger is justified.

Anger thoughts. *This isn't fair. They shouldn't be treating me this way. They're being mean. This is stupid.* Usually anger thoughts involve judgments, thinking what's happening shouldn't be happening or people shouldn't be the way they are.

Activity: Describe Your Anger

Think of a recent time when you've felt angry, and describe the situation:

_____

_____

_____

Body sensations. Take a look at these physical sensations connected to anger, and check off any that you experienced in this situation. Add other sensations that you can recall:

- ☐ Tense or tight muscles, such as clenching fists or jaw

- ☐ Trembling or shaking

- ☐ Racing heart

- ☐ Increased breathing rate

- ☐ Change in body temperature, which might lead to feeling hot or cold

- ☐ Other: _____

Urges and behaviors. Anger usually involves aggression, so you might yell, scream, swear, or say hurtful things to someone, or you might even physically lash out, throw things, or hit or punch things or people (including yourself).

What urges did you notice when you were in the situation you described?

_____

_____

What did you actually do?

_____

_____

Other words for anger. Circle any of these words that describe how you felt in this situation:

Annoyed	Frustrated	Irritated
Exasperated	Resentful	Bitter
Mad	Irate	Furious
Aggravated	Bothered	Enraged
Outraged	Exasperated	Indignant
Impatient		

If you can think of another word or words that fit better, add them here.

_____

_____

It's important to note that just because a feeling is justified doesn't mean you have to act on the urges associated with it. For example, you can feel anger at your parents for setting a curfew and choose not to respond to your urge to shout at them (this will be covered in chapter 7).

Fear and Anxiety

Fear is different from but very related to anxiety. Fear motivates you to act when there's a threat; it triggers the fight-or-flight response in your body, which helps you to survive in a dangerous situation. Fear and anxiety essentially feel the same physically. The main difference between these two emotions is that fear is present focused and related to a specific threat, while anxiety comes up when there's a more general threat that you are worrying about, something that hasn't happened yet and may never happen. Anxiety will also come up when there's something you might reasonably expect to happen and you expect the results to be catastrophic, out of proportion with reality. So, if you're riding your bike or walking down the road and you're thinking the thought *What if I get hit by a car?* you're likely going to feel anxious. If you're doing a presentation at school and you're thinking, *I'm going to make a fool out of myself and fail the whole thing*, you're going to feel anxious. While there are definitely times when fear is justified, there isn't really a time when you *should* feel anxious, or when you can say that your anxiety would be justified, because it involves a fear of something that isn't a real threat—even if it feels that way!

Some anxiety is helpful, however. Without it, you wouldn't be cautious while crossing the road, so you wouldn't see the car as it comes barreling toward you. Without some anxiety, you might do other things that put you more at risk, like walking alone in an unsafe part of town at night. So we're not trying to get rid of it or rid of any emotion, for that matter, since all emotions serve a purpose, but if you have anxiety regularly—or to the extreme, such as having panic attacks—you want to be able to manage it better, instead of letting it control you.

Fear's purpose. Fear comes up when there is a danger to your safety or your well-being or to that of someone you care about.

What it does. Fear is the emotion that causes you to act to protect yourself or others.

Example of when fear is justified. You're riding your bike or walking across the road and a car is speeding right toward you or someone else. Fear is justified because your safety is threatened.

Activity: Describe Your Fear or Anxiety

Think of a recent time when you've felt fearful or anxious, and describe the situation:

_____

_____

_____

Body sensations. Take a look at these physical sensations that can be connected to fear and anxiety, and check off those that you experienced in this situation. Then add any other sensations that you experienced:

☐ Tense or tight muscles (your body preparing you to flee a dangerous situation)

☐ Trembling or shaking muscles

☐ Racing heart

☐ Increased breathing rate

☐ Change in body temperature, which might lead to feeling hot or cold

☐ Other: _____

Urges and behaviors. With fear, urges and behaviors usually involve running away from the threat to protect yourself or the people you care about. With anxiety, this usually means avoiding a situation (like when you decide not to go to class, because you're worried that you'll have a panic attack and make a fool of yourself) or escaping the situation if you're already in it (like leaving class early, because you're feeling anxious).

What urges did you notice when you were in the situation you described?

_____

_____

What did you actually do?

_____

_____

Other words for fear. Circle any of these words that describe how you felt in this situation:

Anxious	Panicky	Terrified
Scared	Afraid	Apprehensive
Nervous	Worried	Dread

Disturbed	Stressed	Tense
Frantic	Overwhelmed	Alarmed
Disconcerted		

If you can think of another word or words that fit better, add them here.

_____

_____

As you recalled your experience of fear or anxiety, did you notice any similarity to what you experienced when feeling angry? The body sensations can be similar. This is why it can be easy to mix up feelings of anxiety and anger!

Sadness

Sadness's purpose. Sadness is the emotion felt when things aren't the way you expected them to be or when you've experienced a loss of some sort.

What it does. This is the emotion that encourages people around you to try to be of help or offer support; it might also motivate you to try to regain what you've lost.

Examples of when sadness is justified. Your best friend is in Europe for six months on a soccer scholarship; you don't get into your first choice of colleges; your significant other breaks up with you. Sadness is justified because you've experienced loss, even if only temporary, and because things aren't as you had expected them to be.

Activity: Describe Your Sadness

Think of a recent time when you've felt sad, and describe the situation:

_____

_____

_____

Body sensations. Take a look at these physical sensations connected to sadness, and check off the ones you experienced in this situation. Then add any other sensations that you experienced:

☐ Tightness in chest or throat

☐ Heaviness in chest or heart

☐ Tears in eyes

☐ Slumped posture

☐ Tired or heavy body

☐ Other: _____

Urges and behaviors. Feeling sad usually involves withdrawing from others and isolating.

What urges did you notice when you were in the situation you described?

_____

_____

What did you actually do?

_____

_____

Other words for sadness. Circle any of these words that describe how you felt in this situation:

Disappointed	Discouraged	Distraught
Resigned	Hopeless	Miserable
Despair	Grief	Sorrow
Anguish	Down	Distressed
Heartbroken	Glum	

If you can think of another word or words that fit your feelings better, add them here.

_____

_____

Guilt

We often feel guilt and shame in the same situations, and many aspects of these emotions are similar. These two emotions are very common for people engaging in self-harming and self-destructive behaviors, and shame especially can be very powerful in keeping the cycle of a target behavior going. Shame is a little different from guilt and will be covered next.

Guilt's purpose. Guilt is the feeling that comes up when you've done something that goes against your morals and values and you judge your behavior.

What it does. Guilt comes up to help you make amends and to prevent you from acting like this in the future.

Examples of when guilt is justified. You say something to hurt your sister during an argument, and later you think, *That was a low blow. I shouldn't have said that.* You lie to your parents or cheat on a test, and there's part of you (your wise self) that knows the behavior doesn't match with your morals or values, and so you feel guilty about it.

Activity: Describe Your Guilt

Think of a recent time when you've felt guilt and describe the situation here:

_____

_____

_____

Body sensations. Take a look at these body sensations connected to guilt, and check off the ones that you experienced in this situation. Then add any other sensations that you experienced:

☐ Feeling and acting jittery, nervous

☐ Hot, flushed face

☐ Bowed head

☐ Other: _____

Urges and behaviors. When feeling guilty, you often want to make amends (apologizing to your sister, for example) to try to make up for what you did.

What urges did you notice when you were in the situation you described?

_____

_____

What did you actually do?

_____

_____

Other words for guilt. Circle any of these words that describe how you felt in this situation:

Remorseful   Apologetic

Regretful   Sorry

If you can think of another word or words that fit your feelings better, add them here.

_____

_____

Shame

Shame's purpose. Shame protects you by keeping you connected to others. Shame comes up when you've done something or when there is something about you as a person that could cause a person (or group of people) to reject you if they knew about it.

What it does. Shame causes you to hide—either yourself or your behavior—so that you can remain connected to people who are important to you. Shame is also the emotion that comes up to try to stop you from doing the same behavior again. If people know about your behavior, shame causes you to try to make amends in those relationships.

Examples of when shame is justified. You cut yourself, and you hide the cuts so that others won't reject you for this behavior. Whether or not shame is justified in this example depends on who you're hiding from: some people might reject you for cutting, in which case shame is justified; it's causing you to hide the behavior, protecting you by keeping you connected. But others (like your parents, your best friend, or your therapist) may not reject you, in which case shame would not be justified.

You may also experience this emotion if there's something about you that makes you different from others, or at least you believe it makes you different. This could be your sexuality or gender identity, a mental health or addiction problem, your religion, or a particular belief or opinion you hold. Hiding that part of yourself protects you from being rejected by others. It's sometimes difficult to tell whether shame is justified or not, because it involves an evaluation of others and what they might think if they knew about this thing.

More often than not, shame isn't justified. It often comes up, though, because shame is the awful, soul-sucking feeling that we feel when we judge ourselves. So instead of thinking, *I shouldn't have said that to my sister*, you're now thinking, *What kind of person am I that I would say that to my sister?* or *I'm awful.* Judging yourself for something you've done or for something you feel is defective or wrong about you will cause you to feel shame.

One reason you may tend to confuse guilt and shame is that you can feel both at the same time, when you judge your behavior and you judge yourself for having done that behavior. If this idea of shame resonates with you, hold on to that idea, because chapters 6 and 7 will give you more skills to help reduce these painful feelings.

Activity: Describe Your Shame

Think of a recent time when you've felt shame, and describe the situation here:

_____

_____

_____

Body sensations. Take a look at these physical sensations connected to shame, and check off the ones you experienced in this situation. Then add any other sensations that you experienced:

- ☐ Pain in the pit of the stomach

- ☐ Slumped posture, bowed head

- ☐ Hot, flushed face

- ☐ Sense of dread

- ☐ Difficulty making eye contact

- ☐ Other: _____

Urges and behaviors. Shame can make you want to crawl under the nearest rock; it can be difficult to make eye contact. It can create an urge to hide from others and isolate yourself.

What urges did you notice when you were in the situation you described?

_____

_____

What did you actually do?

_____

_____

Other words for shame. Circle any of these words that describe how you felt in this situation:

Mortified

Self-loathing

Self-disgust

If you can think of another word or words that fit your feelings better, add them here.

_____

_____

There aren't really many other words for shame, although sometimes we use the words "embarrassed" or "humiliated," which are both very different from shame. You can think of *embarrassed* as the feeling you have when you walk out of the bathroom with TP stuck to your foot—embarrassing situations we can usually laugh at later. Humiliation is a little closer to shame, but it also involves anger—the sense of someone having caused you to feel shame when you didn't deserve it.

Activity: Which Emotion Is It, Anyway?

To practice accurately labeling feelings, read through the following stories and circle which emotions you think would be justified in each situation. (Answers are at the end of this exercise.)

1. Hallie recently starting dating someone at school. This was her first relationship, and she found out that this person was still on an online dating site when they had already agreed that they weren't going to see other people.

    Anger   Fear   Sadness   Guilt   Shame

2. Silas was at a party where a bunch of his friends decided that going for a swim would be a good idea. Everyone had been drinking alcohol, and one of his friends who couldn't swim got pulled into the pool by accident. Fortunately, she was able to make it to the edge of the pool where others helped her out, but seeing this happen freaked Silas out. He started thinking about how disappointed his parents would be if they could see him and that maybe these weren't people he should be spending his time with.

Anger   Fear   Sadness   Guilt   Shame

3. Nevaeh tried out for the school play. She had never done this before, but she wanted to do some extracurricular activities and thought this would be a good place to start. She had spent a lot of time rehearsing for the audition, and when she found out that she hadn't made it into the cast, she couldn't help thinking that this was an opportunity she would have really enjoyed. She could see that the people who'd been picked for the play were the same old popular kids. It wasn't fair.

Anger   Fear   Sadness   Guilt   Shame

4. Jenson had another fight with his parents. They were always getting down on him for not doing well in school, and they just didn't seem to understand how hard it was for him. During their fight, he said some really hurtful things to them, which wasn't like him and wasn't who he wanted to be, but he was just so frustrated.

Anger   Fear   Sadness   Guilt   Shame

Answer key: 1. Anger, sadness. 2. Anger, fear, guilt. 3. Anger, sadness. 4. Anger, guilt, shame.

Hopefully, you're getting better at naming your own emotions. The next worksheet is going to help you walk through the experience of an intense emotion, so you can get a better sense of what this is like for you. First, here's an example of how Goldie did this:

Sample Worksheet: Goldie's Emotions

Date: *July 30*

Description of situation: *My sisters were teasing me. They know this is a trigger for me, but they do it anyway. I tried to practice skills: I asked them to stop and told them I was getting angry, but they wouldn't stop. I felt tears come into my eyes, and I got up and left.*

Emotion names: *Anger, hurt, shame*

Thoughts: *They're being idiots; I'm telling them they're hurting me, and they won't stop. They obviously don't care. I'm going to lose it, and then I'm the one who's going to get in trouble. I'm using my skills, and it's not working. This is stupid.*

Body sensations: *Tension in my body, clenched fists, racing heart, blushing, slumped posture, looking away from everyone.*

Urges: *To cry, to yell at them to shut up, to cut myself.*

Behaviors: *I told them they were hurting me and asked them to stop. When they didn't stop, I got up and left.*

Looking back on the situation now from your wise self, were the emotions justified? Why or why not?

Anger and hurt were justified, because they were saying things on purpose to hurt me, and they were preventing me from having a good time. Also, I feel excluded when they gang up on me. Shame wasn't warranted, because I didn't do anything to cause them to reject me. I think I was feeling ashamed because I was feeling rejected and because I was judging myself for feeling so hurt.

Notice that after describing the situation and what happened, Goldie looked at whether her emotions were justified. And she noticed that her feeling of shame was not justified.

Worksheet: Getting to Know Your Emotions

Think of a recent time when you've had some intense feelings. Record when it happened and describe the situation. Then name the emotions you felt, your thoughts, body sensations, urges, and behaviors. Finally, ask your wise self if your emotions in the situation were justified and why or why not.

Date: _____

Description of situation: _____

_____

_____

Emotion name(s): _____

Thoughts: _____

_____

_____

Body sensations: _____

_____

Urges: _____

_____

Behaviors: _____

_____

Looking back on the situation now from your wise self, was the emotion(s) justified? Why or why not?

_____

_____

_____

So, how'd you do? Who knew figuring out what you're feeling could be so much work, right? And, of course, this is only half the work; the other half is practice. It's important to practice noticing your emotions and all the parts of those emotions, like you've done here. The worksheet you've just completed will help; visit http://www.newharbinger.com/45458 to download copies of this worksheet to do more with this. I'd suggest filling one out whenever you have an intense emotion over the next couple of weeks. This will help you practice labeling your emotions more accurately and might help you see more connections between those painful feelings and your target behavior.

And good news: some of the tools you've been using already will help you get more familiar with those emotions. These include the forward bend, sticking your face in cold water, and paced breathing (to help you get reregulated, so you can think again), and mindfulness. Remember, when you're being mindful, you're focusing on one thing at a time, in the present moment, with your full attention, and with acceptance. This is going to help you get better at noticing when you're feeling something, and by tuning into the thoughts, urges, and body sensations, you'll have more information to help you figure out what that emotion is. Remember that when you can name the emotion, you're going to be in a better position to use the skills still to come to help you tame the emotion.

Wrapping Up

In this chapter, you've done a lot of hard work on figuring out your emotions. You've looked at some of the more painful emotions that tend to play an important role in self-harming and self-destructive behaviors. If these five emotions don't really resonate with you as feeding into your target behavior, you'll need to do some additional reading about other emotions, but chances are you've been able to recognize at least one emotion that's contributing to your target behavior, so that gives you a place to start.

In the next chapter, you'll begin using some mindfulness skills to become more accepting of yourself, others, situations, and your emotions. Doing this will help you learn how to not increase your emotional pain when you are experiencing difficult emotions.

Chapter 6

Stop Adding Fuel to the Fire

Have you ever noticed how things that you do can make your emotions more intense? Like venting to your friends, rehashing or complaining about a situation, and expressing your feelings, usually anger related, about it. We all do this at times, and most of us will say it makes us feel better, but if you pay close attention, you'll find it has you reliving the painful situation, emotions and all, which usually ends up making you feel worse. One reason for this is that complaining about something keeps us focused on it for longer. It's hard to forget about an annoyance while you're grumbling about it.

This chapter offers three skills to help you not add more fuel to the emotional fire; these skills are being nonjudgmental, reality acceptance, and self-validation (Linehan 1993). Keep in mind that these skills won't get rid of feelings altogether—none of the skills do that, since all emotions serve a purpose. But there are certainly things you can do to prevent extra emotional pain from coming up, and when there's less there, it's more manageable, meaning that you won't have to go to extremes to tolerate it, and you're one step closer to leaving those target behaviors behind.

Sadie's Story

Sadie's parents divorced when she was five years old. Her dad remarried (a Cinderella story without the fun parts), and Sadie had mostly lived with her mom after that. Unfortunately, her mother struggled with emotional problems herself, and Sadie had heard her mother talk about killing herself more than once, mostly when they were fighting. They fought often, and Sadie had learned that it was safest not to share her feelings with her mother, so she stuffed them inside. As Sadie got older, she learned to turn to cutting to help her deal with her feelings, and as a teen she learned that drinking alcohol and smoking cannabis helped her numb out for a while. Sleep also became a favorite pastime. By tenth grade, Sadie had pretty much stopped going to school, because she had been so depressed and anxious, but she was trying to get her life back on track and started seeing a therapist who was teaching her DBT skills to help her manage her emotions.

The first goal Sadie had been working on in therapy was attending just one class every day, in an attempt to save something of her school year. In working on this, she and her therapist were able to see a pattern. Sadie would wake up in the morning with the best of intentions to get herself to class, but then her anxiety would kick in, and she would start to judge herself: What is wrong with me? Every other kid goes to school, and it's not a big deal. I should be able to get up and go. I'm so useless. *Sadie was not only feeling anxious now but also feeling angry at herself and ashamed. Then her thoughts would spiral even further:* It's not fair that I have to work so hard when everyone else has it so easy. My friends didn't grow up having to deal with all of this garbage. Why couldn't I have had a normal childhood, with parents who actually took care of me, instead of me having to take care of them? *This triggered even more emotion for Sadie: anger at her parents and then guilt and more shame for having these thoughts. She knew that her parents had done the best they could with what they had, and it wasn't their fault that they couldn't give her what she needed. In the end, Sadie would go through her usual ritual of self-harm, and then crawl back into bed to escape her thoughts and feelings.*

As you can see, there was a lot going on here for Sadie. Can you relate? The good news is there are skills that can help with all of this. The first is the skill of being nonjudgmental.

Being Nonjudgmental

Being nonjudgmental will help prevent you from getting overwhelmed with the extra emotions that judgments often trigger and will help you prevent yourself from turning to self-harm or other target behaviors. For example, when Sadie thinks to herself that her friends didn't have to put up with all of this "garbage" when they were growing up, this judgmental word probably triggers more emotion (probably anger related) in Sadie; this will make it more likely that she'll struggle with intense emotions, which will increase the likelihood of her self-harming. Noticing when she is being judgmental will gradually help Sadie stop triggering these intense emotions and decrease the possibility of self-harm.

You may have a lot of questions already—if so, be sure to take it slowly, because this is a tough skill! Let me break this down further for you, starting with what I mean by *judgment*.

What Is a Judgment?

Think of a judgment as a short form label you use to describe people (including yourself), situations, or things. To be clear, I'm talking about the judgments you say out loud as well as the ones you just think to yourself, since what happens in your head also influences your emotions and behaviors. Examples of judgments would be *wrong*, *bad*, *stupid*, *ugly*, *ridiculous*, and *awful*. There are problems with judgments. First, these labels don't provide useful information: what "wrong" or "bad" means to one person may not be the same for the next person. By telling someone their behavior is "wrong," you're not telling them specifically what you want them to do differently so that you would no longer see their behavior as being wrong. A second problem with judgments is that they make it harder for you to see reality as it really is—in other words, it's typical to think about these judgments as though they were the truth, or facts, when they're not.

Sadie's thinking *I'm useless* is a perfect example: if Sadie were to say to her friend, "I'm so useless," without filling in the rest of the story, the friend would likely have no clue why on earth Sadie was saying this; the judgment doesn't provide any helpful information. Calling herself *useless* also triggers more pain for Sadie, weighing her down even more, and because it's typical for any of us to believe what we think, calling herself *useless* makes it likely that Sadie will act as though she were incapable of going to school—what's the point in trying if she's useless? This is why judgments are so damaging.

It's important to understand that being nonjudgmental doesn't mean you have to be positive all the time, and it doesn't mean having no opinions. It means you take the judgmental words out and you replace them with what you really mean (the long version instead of the short judgmental labels). This long version includes the facts of the situation and your feelings about it; feelings are nonjudgmental, so if you *like* something or if you *dislike* or *hate* something, it's not a judgment—it's your feeling. This next exercise will help you understand what a judgment is.

Activity: Judgment vs. Nonjudgment

Read each of the following statements and decide whether the statement is a judgment or a nonjudgment. Circle your answer.

1. *Cutting isn't a healthy way of dealing with emotions.*

   Judgment   Nonjudgment

2. *I'm such an awful person for calling my parents names.*

   Judgment   Nonjudgment

3. *I feel hurt because my friend didn't invite me to her graduation party.*

   Judgment   Nonjudgment

4. *I didn't get high enough grades to get into the college I wanted, and I am so disappointed.*

   Judgment   Nonjudgment

5. *I was lazy in school this year and got awful grades.*

   Judgment   Nonjudgment

6. *It's not a wise choice for me to drink alcohol, because it makes it harder for me to manage my emotions.*

   Judgment   Nonjudgment

7. *Tom Holland is an amazing actor!*

   Judgment   Nonjudgment

8. *I'm so angry that my math teacher gave me detention today for texting during class!*

   Judgment   Nonjudgment

9. *It's not safe to send pictures of myself to others.*

   Judgment   Nonjudgment

10. *I was so stupid for quitting my job when I was feeling angry.*

    Judgment   Nonjudgment

Answer key: 1. Nonjudgment. 2. Judgment. 3. Nonjudgment. 4. Nonjudgment. 5. Judgment. 6. Nonjudgment. 7. Judgment. 8. Nonjudgment. 9. Nonjudgment. 10. Judgment.

Hopefully, you're seeing what I mean by judgment and nonjudgment, but this skill typically takes some time to learn and develop. Understanding will come with practice, but it can help to have conversations with someone (like your wise person or someone who is supporting you in this work you're doing). It also takes a lot of practice to start changing these judgments to nonjudgments.

Keep in mind that you're not trying to eliminate judgments altogether. Doing so is pretty impossible, and trying to do it can trap you in a cycle where you end up judging yourself for not being fully nonjudgmental. Not every judgmental thought is going to be problematic—for example, judging someone as "weird" when they're wearing shorts in cold weather probably isn't going to trigger much emotional pain for you, and noticing that the cheese in your fridge has gone "bad" is probably not going to throw you into your emotion mind. Right now, though, it's going to be helpful if you can work on being aware of when you're judging. Then you'll have the option of using this skill, if you choose, to reduce judgmental thoughts when they prove problematic.

So how do you do notice when you're judging? A good clue is when your anger emotions (annoyance, irritation, frustration, anger, rage, and so on) start to escalate. When you notice this, or if your wise self recognizes that you're feeling more intense emotions than what seems to be warranted in the situation, there's a good chance you're judging. You can also practice this mindfulness exercise to help you increase your awareness of judgmental thoughts.

Activity: The Gatekeeper

Sitting in a comfortable position, start by just noticing your breath: breathing in, breathing out, slowly, deeply, and comfortably. After a few moments of focusing on your breath, bring your attention to your thoughts and emotions. Imagine yourself standing at the gate of a castle. You are in charge of who comes and goes through that door—you are the gatekeeper—but instead of people coming through the gate, your thoughts and feelings are coming through (you also might notice physical sensations at times).

The idea here isn't that you're going to decide which thoughts and feelings get to come in; if they come to the door, they need to be let in, or they'll start to bang on the door harder and harder. Instead, you just greet each thought and feeling and allow it to enter, acknowledging its presence before moving on to the next. In other words, you accept each experience as it comes—*Here's a judgmental thought*, *Here's an anxious thought*, *Here comes sadness*, *Here is a thought about the past*, *Here comes another judgment*, and so on. As you note each experience and acknowledge what is coming up for you, the thought or emotion will pass through the gate and go on its way rather than hang around. It might come back again (and again), but you'll see that it doesn't stay long; it just passes through, and then the next experience arises.

You don't have to do this mindfulness practice for very long. I'd suggest no more than two minutes, especially to start—it can be quite hard!—but the more you practice this, or other mindfulness exercises that have you noticing and accepting your internal experiences (thoughts, emotions, physical sensations), the more you'll be able to pick up on those judgmental thoughts when they arise.

How to Reduce Your Judging

Once you're aware of when you're being judgmental, and you want to work on being nonjudgmental, you have two choices. The first choice is to just let it go. And when I say "just," I don't mean to make it sound easy, but sometimes you can notice the judgment and decide you don't need or want to judge. For example, think of a post you see on Instagram that you think is *stupid*—of course, that's a judgment. Hopefully, you'll notice the judgment and decide to drop it (for example, saying to yourself, *That's a judgment, I'm going to just let it go*). Sometimes you can do that, especially if you're not emotionally attached to the person or thing you're judging, but often it's not so simple, and that's when you can choose to put some effort into changing the language you're using. This is the second way to work on being non-judgmental. You do this by taking out the judgmental label (in this case, *stupid*) and replacing it with the facts of the situation and your feelings.

Activity: Turning Judgments into Nonjudgments

For each of the judgmental statements below, take the judgment out and turn it into a nonjudgmental statement. First state the facts of the situation and your feelings about it, and then combine the two to make a nonjudgmental statement. Here's an example: You see a meme your friend Ash posted on Instagram making fun of a certain sexual identity. Your first (judgmental) thought might be, *That Instagram post is stupid.*

What are the facts? *Ash posted a meme that puts down transgender people.*

What are your feelings? *I find the meme offensive, and I feel angry that Ash posted it.*

Nonjudgmental statement: *I disagree with what Ash posted. I find it offensive, and it makes me angry. Or, I feel angry that Ash posted this meme. I wish Ash wouldn't be disrespectful of other people's identities.*

Now it's your turn.

1. You get a grade that is lower than usual for you, and you think, *I'm so useless.*

   What are the facts? _____

   What are your feelings? _____

   Nonjudgmental statement: _____

   _____

2. Your friend finds out you've been cutting, and she tells your mom. You think, *She's an awful friend, I hate her!*

   What are the facts? _____

   What are your feelings? _____

Nonjudgmental statement: _____

_____

3. Now think of a judgment you noticed yourself making recently; the judgment could be of yourself, someone else, or a situation more generally. What's your judgmental thought?

_____

_____

What are the facts? _____

What are your feelings? _____

Nonjudgmental statement: _____

_____

Do you notice a difference in your feelings? If so, make some notes here about how they changed:

_____

_____

_____

Remember not to expect the emotions to disappear altogether. Usually this skill helps reduce the intensity of your feeling (for example, you might be frustrated with yourself instead of angry about your grade), or it might change one painful feeling to another less painful feeling (you might feel guilt instead of shame about getting a lower grade than usual).

By the way, if you're starting to notice that you judge a lot, welcome to the human race! (Now do your best to not judge yourself for judging!) We tend to be judgmental creatures, but this is a learned habit that you can change if you put the work in. Some people have a greater tendency to judge themselves, and this is especially common for people who self-harm: you might notice that your self-judgments often trigger emotions like anger toward yourself, shame, and self-disgust, which contribute to your self-harming or self-destructive behavior; turning to your target behavior triggers more emotions; and you get stuck in a vicious cycle. Does this sound familiar? Are you especially hard on yourself? Do you bully or verbally abuse yourself? If so, reducing self-judgment will be helpful, and even if you don't think you judge yourself that often, I would strongly encourage you to work on doing it less. We can never be too compassionate toward ourselves.

Self-Judgments

There are some common themes among self-judgments. For example, you might think you're a *bad person*, that you're *stupid* or *useless* when it comes to school, or that you're *ugly*. The first option I mentioned earlier, of letting these kinds of judgments go, is usually pretty hard when you notice yourself doing this, because self-judgments like these are likely to have a lot of emotion attached to them, and this makes them stickier. These are the judgments that you are more likely to believe are facts, and it can be hard to see them as judgmental thoughts. But it's worth the effort. Here's how Sadie changed her self-judgments to nonjudgmental statements, using the same method as in the previous activity.

1. What is a judgmental statement you say to yourself on a regular basis? *There's something wrong with me.*

2. What are the facts that cause you to judge yourself this way? You can generalize or use one specific example. *I don't go to school like other kids. I cut myself.*

3. What are the emotions that cause you to judge yourself this way? *Shame, anger at myself, disappointment in myself.*

4. Now write some statements to turn your self-judgment into nonjudgments:

   - *I feel ashamed that I can't manage to go to school regularly and that I cut myself to try to deal with my feelings.*

   - *I think I'm different from the other kids at school because of the emotional problems I have, and this makes me feel ashamed and angry at myself.*

   - *I'm disappointed in myself for not reaching my goals of going to one class every day and reducing my cutting.*

Notice that Sadie isn't trying to turn her self-judgments into positive statements. Most of us would have a hard time turning a long-standing judgment like this into a positive statement. Instead, she's stating the facts as they are and her emotions. This is a nonjudgmental stance.

Activity: Changing Your Self-Judgments

Change your self-judgments to a nonjudgmental statement by answering these questions:

1. What is a judgmental statement you say to yourself on a regular basis?

   _____

   _____

2. What are the facts that cause you to judge yourself this way? You can generalize like Sadie did, or you can use a specific example.

   _____

   _____

3. What are the emotions that cause you to judge yourself this way?

   _____

   _____

4. Now write some statements to turn your self-judgment into nonjudgments:

   _____

   _____

   _____

   _____

Hopefully, you were able to come up with at least a couple of nonjudgmental statements for your judgmental thoughts. If not, you might be in your emotional or reasoning self right now, which can get in the way of finding a more balanced, wise perspective. If you couldn't come up with even one nonjudgment, you can come back to this another time when you might be in your wise self, and try again. Here's something else that might help: imagine if your best friend, sibling, or even a pet were saying this judgmental thing to themselves, what would you tell them?

_____

_____

It can also help to imagine if your best friend, sibling, or your pet knew you were talking to yourself this way. What would they say to you?

_____

_____

If you're still struggling with this, you might need to ask for some help from your wise person or someone else you trust. This can be a really tough exercise, especially when you're not used to being compassionate to yourself. But as long as you continue to judge yourself, you risk triggering extra emotional pain, which will keep you stuck in a vicious cycle with your target behavior.

Once you've written out your nonjudgmental statements, the next step is practice, of course! Make a photocopy of your statements, or take a picture of them and keep them on your phone or tablet, so you have them with you. Then, throughout the day, when you notice your old self-judgmental talk coming up, bring out your list to help you respond to it. You should also read these statements to yourself, outside of any problematic situations, to practice them. The more you practice, the better you'll get at talking to yourself in this kinder, more compassionate way.

Speaking of kindness, the following loving-kindness mindfulness practice (Brantley and Hanauer 2008) can help you reduce your judgments and bring compassion to yourself and to others. It will be helpful to find a quiet place to do this practice, where you can sit for a while without being disturbed.

Activity: Loving-Kindness Practice

Sitting in a comfortable position, bring your attention to your breath, becoming aware of the movement of your body as you breathe. You don't have to change your breathing, but just notice the physical sensations, perhaps noticing your belly rising and falling as you breathe, or maybe noticing the feel of air as it enters and exits your nostrils as you inhale and exhale. Just be with your breath. When distracting thoughts arise, notice them without judgment and return your attention to your breath.

Now bring to mind someone for whom you have feelings of love. This might be a family member, your best friend, or a pet; it could be someone from your present or your past. Seeing or feeling this person in your mind, notice your feelings of love or caring for them arise within your body. You may feel a smile spreading across your face, or perhaps you feel a warmth in your chest; whatever it is, just allow yourself to feel it. Now, letting go of this person in your imagination, but holding on to the awareness of the feelings that have arisen, bring yourself to mind, and see if you can offer loving-kindness to yourself by allowing these words to become your words. You can say these aloud or to yourself:

May I be happy

May I be healthy

May I ride the waves of my life

May I live in peace

No matter what I am given.

Notice the feelings that arise within you, and just allow them to be, repeating those words again.

When you're ready, see if you can offer loving-kindness to someone who you know loves you and supports you. Bringing this person to mind, perhaps seeing their face in your imagination, focus on sending them loving-kindness by repeating these words:

May you be happy

May you be healthy

May you ride the waves of your life

May you live in peace

No matter what you are given.

Once your feelings flow easily to this loved one, turn your attention to someone with whom you have some difficulty; it's best not to start with the most difficult person in your life, but bring to mind someone who evokes feelings of irritation, frustration, or annoyance. As you bring this person to mind and hold them in your awareness, see if you can send loving-kindness their way by repeating these words:

May you be happy

May you be healthy

May you ride the waves of your life

May you live in peace

No matter what you are given.

Notice whatever sensations and feelings arise within you, and do your best to just allow them to be.

Finally, bring to mind a community to which you feel connected: your family, classmates, neighbors, or maybe even including all beings on the planet; and include yourself in this offering of loving-kindness if you can. Then repeat these words:

May we be happy

May we be healthy

May we ride the waves of our lives

May we live in peace

No matter what we are given.

Notice the sensations and feelings that arise within you; allow yourself to sit with these for a few moments until you're ready to end the practice.

What was this practice like for you? Sometimes people find it difficult to bring loving-kindness to themselves. If it was really difficult, next time try starting out with someone who you know cares about you, and you can work your way up to sending loving-kindness to yourself last. Or maybe you struggled with sending loving-kindness to the difficult person in your life. If so, you may need to switch to a less difficult person! Whatever the case, rest assured that, as with any new skill, the loving-kindness practice will come more naturally over time.

You may have noticed that the skill of being nonjudgmental is very much about the language you use and how it can trigger extra emotional pain for you. Remember, you don't have to eliminate judgments, but being aware of when you're judging allows you to choose whether you want to work on changing this to reduce your emotional pain. Now let's take a broader look at not judging—or acceptance—with the skill of accepting reality as it is.

Reality Acceptance

Reality acceptance is about accepting or acknowledging reality as it is (Linehan 1993). Acceptance doesn't mean approving of, liking, or being okay with something. Because reality acceptance involves not judging, you're already working on this with the skill you've just learned—and, by the way, you've already been working on both of these skills in the form of mindfulness, since being nonjudgmental and acceptance are part of being mindful! But accepting reality is a broader skill where you focus on bringing a more accepting attitude to whatever past or present reality you're fighting.

Activity: How Acceptance Helps

Think of a difficult situation in your life that you believe you've already accepted, either a past situation (for example, when you moved to a new neighborhood or when a relationship ended) or something that is presently happening (maybe your parents are going through a separation, or you're struggling with making friends at school). Whatever the situation is, it was painful when it first happened (or started), but now you've accepted it; you've been able to let it go and moved on. Other examples of difficult-to-accept situations might be when someone you loved died, losing a relationship that was important to you, or not getting something you really wanted (like a job, a part in a school play, or a position on a school team). Write a brief description of your situation here:

_____

_____

Next, think about how you felt in that situation in the past—or, if you're still in this situation, think about how you felt at first—and compare that to how you feel about the situation now that you've accepted it. What changed about your experience once you got to acceptance? Make some notes here:

_____

_____

People will often say that they felt a sense of relief, or "lighter," like a weight had been lifted, once they accepted their situation. Sometimes they feel like the situation has less power or control over them, so they think about it less often now, and when they do still think about it, it's less painful and they can see it more clearly. Perhaps you notice a sense of feeling more at peace, being calmer about the situation, and spending less energy on it. This is how reality acceptance helps—when you're dealing with self-harming and self-destructive behaviors, this is another skill that will help you have less emotional pain and move away from those target behaviors.

Fighting Reality vs. Accepting Reality

Now that you have a sense of what this skill is going to do for you, let's look more closely at what it means. Accepting reality is the opposite of *fighting reality*. Sadie's thoughts of *Why me?* are a great example of how we often fight reality. She was thinking it was unfair that she had to grow up the way she did and that her parents should have taken better care of her. This is fighting reality. Remember, I'm not saying that Sadie should like or be okay with things as they are (or as they were, in the case of her difficult past), but when she fights reality (essentially by judging reality), she's triggering more pain for herself.

Activity: What Are You Not Accepting?

Think about how this skill applies to you. What realities are you fighting in your life that are contributing to ongoing pain and probably to the target behaviors you're working on? Make a list in the space provided of things you think you need to accept—and if you need more room, grab another piece of paper and keep writing!

_____

_____

_____

_____

_____

What does fighting reality look like for you? Looking back at Sadie's story, you can see that she would get stuck in dwelling, blaming, self-harm, using drugs and alcohol, and sleeping. Target behaviors are often a way of fighting reality: _If I do this [target behavior], I won't have to acknowledge this is my reality. I cannot think about it, so I need to escape or avoid it._ Sound familiar? In the space provided, write your thoughts about what you do to fight reality:

_____

_____

_____

_____

_____

Avoiding difficult emotions is a very human response: like all creatures, we try to avoid the things that cause us pain, and for humans, this includes both emotional and physical pain. Unfortunately, avoiding an emotion doesn't work as well as avoiding something that causes physical pain. For example, you probably learned not to touch the stove as a kid, to avoid getting burned, and that behavior keeps you safe. However, avoiding difficult emotions not only fails to solve the problem but usually causes more pain. That's because avoidance causes your world to shrink over time; the more you avoid, the more you learn to fear the thing you're avoiding, which causes more avoidance, and so on. When you continue to avoid, you don't learn healthy ways of coping, and instead you learn to rely on unhealthy coping mechanisms, like self-harm, substance use, and other target behaviors. That's why it's so important to break the cycle of avoidance through reality acceptance.

You've already taken the first step in this skill, which is being more aware: noticing what you're not accepting and noticing what nonacceptance looks like for you, which likely includes your target behaviors. Now that you know what you need to work on, here's how you do it.

Steps to Reality Acceptance

Step 1: Choose what you're going to work on accepting. To start with, please don't choose the most difficult situation in your life, but choose something that's less painful to get more comfortable with practicing this skill. You can work your way up to the more painful stuff later. Then make the commitment to yourself: *As of right now, I'm going to practice accepting [fill in the blank].*

Step 2: Notice when you are not acknowledging your reality but are fighting or judging that reality instead. Write down some of the fighting reality thoughts you're noticing, such as *It's not fair, It shouldn't be this way,* or *This is stupid.*

Step 3: Turn your mind back to acceptance. Remind yourself why you want to accept this reality, and how acceptance will help. You may want to remember what it was like to have accepted something in the past, as this will help motivate you to practice this skill now.

Then repeat steps 2 and 3 over and over again: notice when you're fighting your reality, and then turn your mind back to acceptance. I call this the *internal argument,* and it's a normal part of the process of accepting—you will waffle back and forth!

When you're working on reality acceptance, it can be helpful to write out statements ahead of time that you can read to yourself when you notice you are falling back into fighting reality. These statements will gradually help you change your thinking about the painful situation, helping you make the shift from fighting reality to acknowledging this is how it is. Look at the statements that Sadie wrote to help her accept her past:

- *The past is in the past, and I can't go back and change it. I want to work on accepting my past, so it doesn't continue to limit my future.*

- *My parents weren't able to give me what I needed when I was growing up, which has made things more difficult for me now, but I'm doing my best to learn healthy ways of managing my emotions.*

- *I don't want to be like my mom (afraid of emotions and thinking about suicide), so I'm going to work my butt off to be healthier in my life.*

- *I am putting aside what seems "fair" and "not fair" and acknowledging the reality that this is what I had to deal with when I was growing up.*

Activity: Practicing Reality Acceptance

Choose one of the realities you're fighting from the list you made earlier; ideally, make it one of the less painful situations on the list. If it seems impossible right now to choose one—or if you find yourself not willing to work on accepting any of the situations on your list just yet, that's okay—you can choose something else instead (like the fact that your sib never cleans up after themselves, that you're on dish duty tonight, or that your basketball team didn't make the playoffs this year). In the following space, write some statements that will help you stop fighting and instead acknowledge that reality:

_____

_____

_____

_____

As you did with the nonjudgmental statements you wrote to help change your self-judgments, you need to read these statements to yourself regularly to help you turn your fighting reality into acknowledging reality. Keep this list with you, so you can read these statements in response to your fighting-reality thoughts when they arise. Remember steps 2 and 3: notice when you start to fight the reality, and then read your statements to help you turn your mind back to acceptance.

One final note before moving on from reality acceptance: if you choose to accept something, it doesn't mean that you're giving up on trying to change it, and it doesn't mean sitting back and being passive. Acceptance means only that you are acknowledging this is your reality. You can then ask yourself, *Now what am I going to do about it?* And this is where so many of the other skills you've been learning come into play. Therefore, don't let this idea—that acceptance means giving up—get in the way of you choosing to accept.

So far, you've been looking at being nonjudgmental and practicing reality acceptance with specific situations or people (including yourself). Now you're going to learn how to use these skills to help you more directly with your emotions.

Self-Validation: Accepting Your Emotions

Many of us have at least one emotion that we struggle to let ourselves feel and that we judge ourselves for feeling. Some people, like Sadie, struggle with many different emotions. Remember, Sadie learned that it wasn't safe to express her emotions to her mom, who was her main person, so she was stuffing many of the emotions she was feeling. Stuffing, or pushing away, typically involves judgment; although you might not be judging consciously, you're still telling yourself, *It's not okay to have this experience.* Another word for this is *self-invalidation*.

It's important to accept all of your emotions, because when you judge or invalidate yourself for feeling something, you end up creating more emotional pain for yourself. Again looking at Sadie, you can see how she was judging herself for feeling anxious, and this caused her to feel ashamed and angry at herself, which made her pain a whole lot worse. Remember that accepting something doesn't mean you like it; it just means acknowledging its existence. In the case of emotions, when you can acknowledge or validate that this is how you feel, the feeling typically won't go away, but it won't turn into something stronger, either. And that means that you're going to be more likely to get to your wise self—so you can figure out if there's something you can do to help reduce the pain you're in—rather than react from your emotional self and return to those old target behaviors.

Activity: What Emotions Do You Need to Accept?

What emotions do you judge yourself for feeling? For example, do you tell yourself that you have nothing to be depressed about? Or maybe that it's silly for you to feel anxious? Or perhaps you regularly judge yourself as a drama queen, telling yourself that you're overreacting for feeling hurt or angry? (If you're having trouble figuring this out, it might be helpful to look back at the behavioral analysis you did in chapter 1.) Check off the emotions you think you need to work on accepting:

☐ Anger emotions (including frustration, irritation, annoyance, and rage)

☐ Fear (and fear-related emotions like anxiety, terror, and panic)

☐ Sad emotions (including depression, grief, and disappointment)

☐ Happy emotions (including love, joy, elation, euphoria, and excitement)

☐ Guilt (and guilt-related emotions like remorse, sorrow, and regret)

☐ Shame (including self-disgust and self-loathing)

A caution about validating guilt and shame: If you noted that you need to validate feelings of guilt and shame, I would urge you to look more closely at these two emotions, perhaps revisiting chapter 5 where they were discussed. Often, we feel guilt and shame when we're judging ourselves for having other feelings, and it's important to look for these other emotions rather than just focus on the guilt or shame. Remember Sadie, who was thinking, *There's something wrong with me* for feeling anxious, and this triggered shame in her. If you judge yourself as being *a bad person* or think, *This is wrong, I shouldn't feel this way* when you're feeling angry at someone, you're probably also feeling shame (if you're judging yourself) or guilt (if you're judging the feeling). If instead you can accept that you're feeling angry, neither of these other emotions will arise.

Activity: Validating Your Emotions

Once you've identified which emotions you need to work on validating more, choose one to start with; you don't want to overwhelm yourself by taking on everything at once. Here's how Sadie validated her anxiety:

- *I feel anxious.*

- *It's okay that I feel anxious about going to school; I don't like it, but it is what it is, and I'm working on it.*

- *It makes sense that I feel anxious about going to school, because I've missed so much and it's overwhelming.*

- *I feel anxious. It's uncomfortable, but it's just anxiety, and I know I can deal with it.*

Write down the emotion you're working on validating, and then write some statements to validate it.

Emotion: _____

Validation:

_____

_____

_____

_____

You probably know the homework drill by now: practice, practice, practice. Read these statements to yourself when you hear judgments arise in response to that painful feeling, and read them at other times for more practice. I know it might seem like a lot to do, especially given everything you're working on already, but this is how you change your self-talk.

When You Get Stuck

Being nonjudgmental and accepting of others and yourself, while helpful in the long run, can be pretty hard in the moment, so here's a reminder. When you need to reregulate your emotions, you can do your forward bend or go stick your face in cold water. These skills will help you pause for a second and get to a more willing place where you can practice being nonjudgmental and accepting. Another skill that can help here is taking an open posture (Linehan 1993): unclench your hands, uncross your arms, take some deep breaths, and do whatever you can to loosen up tight muscles; this can help you stop fighting reality and develop a more accepting attitude as you move toward acceptance.

Wrapping Up

In this chapter, you've been working on bringing acceptance to your experience, whatever it is. With these skills—being nonjudgmental, reality acceptance, and validating your emotions—you'll find that you'll stop adding fuel to the fire of your emotions. Again, the feelings won't disappear, but when you have fewer emotions, or less intense emotions, you'll more easily be able to tolerate the pain through healthy means instead of turning to your target behavior. Less emotion also means more easily getting to your wise self, and this will help you move on to the next step, which is looking to see if there's something you can do to reduce your pain.

Before moving on, remember to take your time. This book contains a lot of information and skills that may be new to you, and it's important to give yourself time to absorb and practice what you've learned, rather than rush through. Change doesn't happen overnight, and it will take time to learn new skills to replace the old habits.

Chapter 7

Avoid Avoiding

You've been working on accepting your emotions, your thoughts, and yourself as well as what's going on around you. Although acceptance itself doesn't change your experience, it definitely helps prevent it from becoming more painful. The next step is to stop avoiding things in your life. This chapter offers three skills to help you do this: willingness, acting opposite to the emotion, and being effective.

What Is Avoidance?

When you think about that word—*avoidance*—what comes to mind for you? Is it skipping math class? Trying to spend as little time as possible with your stepparent? Not making eye contact with someone you dislike at school? While these are definitely all examples of avoidance, there are many other things we tend to avoid and ways we avoid. Think back to the stories of the various teens you met earlier in this book: they all turned to forms of self-harming and self-destructive behaviors to avoid thinking painful thoughts and feeling painful emotions.

Basically, all of the target behaviors you've read about in this book can be a way of avoiding and escaping some kind of experience, whether it's something going on around you (like other people demanding things of you or a particular situation you're dealing with that's difficult) or internal experiences that cause you distress, like your thoughts, emotions, and physical sensations. The following story may help you consider what you might be avoiding in your life.

Adrian's Story

Adrian had always felt different, like she didn't belong in her own body. Over the years, Adrian had come to realize this was because, although she looked like a male, she felt like a female. This had been the source of a lot of pain for her throughout her life—people bullying her and her own family not understanding her. Now, at seventeen, she still struggled with the idea of being transgender—*she didn't want to be different; it was confusing, for her and for the people around her. This led to feelings of loneliness, sadness, anxiety, shame, and anger much of the time, to the point that she didn't know what to do with these feelings.*

Although Adrian knew these feelings made sense given her experiences, the pain was hard for her to manage, and so she found ways of avoiding the feelings— cutting and burning herself and using drugs and drinking alcohol to avoid thinking about things. She also discovered that lashing out at people around her was a great way of avoiding getting close to others—that way she didn't risk them finding out about how "defective" she was (she avoided feelings of shame), and getting hurt wasn't an option (she avoided feelings of anxiety). Of course, Adrian realized that this was a double-edged sword—yes, she was protecting herself, but now and then she realized how much she was missing out on by not letting herself have relationships with others.

Now it's your turn to consider how avoidance plays a part in your life.

Activity: What Does Avoidance Look Like for You?

Check off what you avoid, and see if you can provide further information (nonjudgmentally!) about people or a situation you're avoiding. Then check off the emotions associated with what you are avoiding:

☐ A person or people in your life. Who? Why?

_____

_____

☐ A situation that causes you to feel anxiety or another painful emotion. Describe the situation and see if you can label the emotions associated with this:

_____

_____

Emotions you're avoiding:

☐ Anger

☐ Sadness

☐ Fear/anxiety

☐ Guilt

☐ Happiness

☐ Boredom

☐ Love

☐ Lust

☐ Shame

☐ Envy (this is the feeling where you want something someone else has)

☐ Jealousy (this is how you feel when you are worried someone might take someone or something away from you)

What other emotions do you associate with avoiding?

_____

_____

Are there thoughts you are trying to avoid, and are these thoughts about the present, the past, or the future? Check off and write about thoughts that you're avoiding:

☐ The present. What specific things are you trying to not think about?

_____

_____

☐ The past. What specific things are you trying to not think about?

_____

_____

☐ The future. What specific things are you trying to not think about?

_____

_____

Now that you have a better idea of what you avoid in your life, consider how this affects you. What are the positive and negative consequences of your avoidance? If you're not yet sure, you might want to take some time to do a pros and cons chart (see chapter 1).

Pros of Avoiding	Cons of Avoiding
Pros of Not Avoiding	Cons of Not Avoiding

Next come some skills to use when you become aware of your avoidance and hopefully make the choice to do something about it.

Being Willing

Not being willing to have an experience—avoiding it—will often increase the pain you're feeling. Think about it: if you're not willing to feel anxious, for example, and you do everything you can to avoid that feeling, you'll end up having even more emotional pain. The anxiety won't disappear and will probably get stronger, and even if your level of anxiety stays the same, avoidance typically ends up adding other emotions into the mix. Take Adrian as an example. She's afraid that others will reject her and is unwilling to put herself in situations where she might get close to people, but that's causing her to feel lonely and isolated and probably even more anxious over time, since avoidance typically increases anxiety.

Willingness means that we might not like an experience, but we're willing to have it; we're open to it rather than closing ourselves off (May 1982). Willingness means that we try our best with what we've got, even if we're not very hopeful or optimistic about the outcome. It's refusing to give up.

The opposite of willingness is willfulness; we all get willful at times. Sometimes things get too painful, and we don't want to keep putting energy and effort into feeling better; we just want to take a break and pretend everything is fine. For example, sometimes you might think it's just not fair that you have to put so much work into living your life on a daily basis when everyone around you seems to be able to manage things fine. Sound familiar? While understandable, willfulness does get in the way, so you still need to do something to change it. Here are some strategies:

1. Label it. Just recognize that willfulness has arisen, and do your best to not judge it. Accept the reality (it is what it is).

2. Remember these skills from chapter 2: go stick your face in cold water or do a forward bend, and focus on making your exhale longer than your inhale to help you get to a place where you can think more clearly.

3. Open up your posture to get to a more willing place. If you think about how willfulness feels in your body, typically you'll notice your muscles are tense; you're closed off—perhaps your arms are folded across your chest, or your fists are clenched. Willingness is about opening up—unclenching, unfolding. Let your arms hang loosely at your sides and spread your fingers

107

wide, opening up to what in DBT is called *willing hands* (Linehan 2014). Continuing to take some slow, deep breaths will also help you feel more open and willing.

4. Change the expression on your face to change how you feel. Our facial expression actually sends signals to our brain that can either increase or decrease our sense of well-being. The DBT skill of *half smiling* (Linehan 1993) is when you slightly upturn the corners of your mouth, but the trick here is to not force a smile: putting on a fake smile actually has the opposite effect of what you're going for, because it creates tension in the muscles in your face, which sends signals to your brain reducing your sense of well-being. The half smile is so slight (think less than Mona Lisa!) that someone looking at you might not be able to see it; the important part is that you feel it. By the way, this is another skill you'll likely want to practice (use a mirror!) outside of distressing events, so you get the hang of what it is and isn't. Be sure to add this one to your list of crisis survival skills (from chapter 2).

Once you're able to let go of willfulness and get to a more willing place, you'll be able to consider the next skill of acting opposite to your emotion, which will help reduce the intensity of your emotion.

Acting Opposite to Your Emotion

One saying we have in DBT is that "emotions love themselves" (Linehan 1993). In other words, when we have an emotion, it creates urges to keep us acting in ways that will feed into it, causing it to stick around and maybe even become more intense. When you're feeling angry and you lash out, for example, your anger usually stays the same or even increases. When you're feeling anxious about going for a job interview and you cancel it, your anxiety will probably be even worse the next time you're facing this kind of situation. So, if acting on your urge keeps the emotion going, doesn't it make sense that doing the opposite of the urge will help the feeling go down?

This is what the skill of *acting opposite to your emotion* is about: you identify the emotion you're experiencing and the urge that's attached to it; and then you act opposite to the urge (Linehan 1993). In other words, you do the opposite of what the·emotion is telling you to do. Before you can practice this, though, there are some other important things you need to know.

When to Act Opposite

First, acting opposite is a skill you use when you want to reduce your emotion; if that's not your goal, it's not going to work. Often, you'll want to reduce an emotion because it's painful or because you know it's likely to lead you down the path to your target behavior. You might also recognize at times that an emotion is higher than what is warranted by the situation, and so you want it to come down. Sometimes, by the way, you might be okay with the emotion, or even get a sense of satisfaction or some other kind of pleasure out of feeling it, but from your wise self, you recognize that letting yourself stay there isn't effective, and the emotion is going to get in your way, like when you're feeling angry with someone. These are all examples of times when acting opposite will be quite helpful.

Remember that every emotion serves a purpose, so you're not trying to stuff them or ignore them. But when an emotion has come and delivered its message—you now know how you feel about a situation and you're ready to do something about it—the emotion can get in the way of you being able to act skillfully. When an emotion stays really intense, it's usually hard to use your wise self to act in a healthy, skillful way. Using anger as an example, sometimes the intensity of your anger can get in the way of your ability to have a productive conversation with the person you're angry with. Or, if you're feeling really anxious about going to a party, this can get in the way of you going to the party, meeting new people, and having a good time. So if your emotion is no longer helpful and you want to reduce it, then acting opposite will help.

How to Act Opposite

You've already been working on naming your emotion accurately (in chapter 5), and this is the first step to using this skill of acting opposite. Remember, you have to be able to name it to tame it. This also includes validating the emotion (from chapter 6). If you aren't accepting the emotion—giving yourself permission to feel it—you're only going to create more pain for yourself, making it more likely you'll get stuck in your emotional self. Whether you can understand the feeling or not, and whether you think it's justified or not, you have to accept that this is what you feel.

The next step in using this skill is figuring out what the urge is that's attached to the feeling: what's the emotion telling you to do?

Once you've identified and validated the emotion, and noted what urge is coming up for you, the next step is to see if your emotion fits the facts of the situation (Linehan 2014). Turning back to chapter 5 is going to help with this, as you'll need to work on becoming more familiar with the purpose of your emotion. Then you'll be able to ask yourself, *Is this feeling warranted or justified, given the facts of the situation?* You can practice this step by first considering Adrian's situation.

Activity: Do Adrian's Emotions Fit the Facts?

For each situation in Adrian's life, write down whether you think Adrian's emotion was justified or not justified.

1. Adrian is bullied by her peers when they find out that she is considering gender transition, and this causes Adrian to feel angry. Is Adrian's anger justified or not justified?

   _____

2. Adrian's best friend Cam has always been very validating and accepting, but Adrian is worried that Cam will reject her after Adrian transitions. Is Adrian's anxiety justified or not justified?

   _____

3. Adrian has recently started talking to her parents about the idea of transitioning, and they have not been supportive, actually trying to discourage her from starting the process. As a result, Adrian has been feeling more distant from them than ever and is very sad about the distance that has opened up between them. Is Adrian's sadness justified or not justified?

   _____

4. Adrian has been hearing her parents arguing late at night, and she knows many of their disagreements are about her: her dad is actually trying to be supportive, but her mother's religious beliefs prevent her from being able to see Adrian's perspective. Adrian feels guilty about her parents' disagreements. Is Adrian's guilt justified or not justified?

_____

5. Adrian has been hiding her identity struggles from her peers at church, knowing that they couldn't possibly understand given the Bible teachings they've heard their entire life. Adrian is positive that if they knew who she really was, they couldn't possibly accept her. Adrian feels shame in this scenario, fearing rejection by these peers. Is Adrian's shame justified or not justified?

_____

6. Adrian has recently been considering connecting with an LGBTQI+ group; however, her intense shame about her gender identity and mental health problems has prevented her from doing so, even though she knows from her wise self that this group would understand and support her. Is Adrian's shame justified or not justified?

_____

Answer key:

1. Anger should come up when we are being hurt or attacked by others, and Adrian is being hurt or attacked by others, so anger is justified.

2. Fear should come up when our life, our health, or our well-being is threatened, so anxiety is not justified.

3. Sadness should come up when things are not the way we expected or hoped they would be, so sadness is justified.

4. Guilt should come up only when we've done something that goes against our morals or values, so guilt is not justified in this case.

5. Shame should come up to prevent us from potentially being rejected by others who are important to us, so in this instance shame is justified.

6. Since there is little likelihood of Adrian being rejected by this group, in this instance shame is not justified.

Now that you've had some practice figuring out if Adrian's emotions fit the facts and are justified or not, take some time to consider your own feelings in certain situations.

Activity: Does Your Emotion Fit the Facts?

Think of a recent situation in which you had a strong emotion—it could be either pleasurable or painful. Recalling that situation as best as you can, answer the following questions to help you decide if your emotion fit the facts: was it justified?

1. Describe the situation sticking to facts (leave the judgments out!): Who was there? Where? When? Describe what happened:

   _____

   _____

   _____

2. What were you feeling in response to the situation? Focus on the feelings that arose in response to the situation, as best as you can, rather than how you feel about your feelings:

   _____

3. Identify the urge that went along with each emotion (grab another piece of paper if you need more room):

   Feeling 1: _____

   Urge: _____

Feeling 2: _____

Urge: _____

Feeling 3: _____

Urge: _____

4. Now check the facts of the situation to see if your feelings were justified:

Feeling 1: _____

When is this emotion justified? _____

Does it fit the facts? Yes or no? Why? _____

_____

Feeling 2: _____

When is this emotion justified: _____

Does it fit the facts? Yes or no? Why? _____

_____

Feeling 3: _____

When is this emotion justified? _____

Does it fit the facts? Yes or no? _____

_____

If the emotion is justified, it will often be a wise choice to act on what the emotion is telling you to do. For example, if Adrian's fear comes up as she's walking home from school, because she sees a group of people who have bullied her in the past, her fear will keep her safe by having her walk in the opposite direction. Similarly, you might want to act on your urge with anger if it's pushing you to try to make changes to a system that you don't like or that you find discriminatory or oppressive, for example, protesting school policies about the student dress code.

But usually if the emotion is not justified—or if it is justified and you still want to reduce it because it's preventing you from acting skillfully, for example, or because it's just so painful—then you're going to act opposite: do the opposite of what the emotion is telling you to do. Looking back at Adrian's story will help this make sense.

Adrian's Story Continued

Adrian has identified that neither her shame nor her anxiety about going to the LGBTQI+ group is justified. People at the group are not going to bully or assault her (her well-being is not at risk, so her anxiety is not warranted). They're also not going to reject her or kick her out of the group (others are not going to reject her for who she is, so her shame is not warranted); rather, they can relate to her struggles, and will likely understand and support her. Therefore, when Adrian notices the urge (related to her anxiety and shame) to not go to the group, she pushes herself to go anyway. To help with this, because those feelings are so high, she goes in first to speak with one of the counselors. Having one familiar face in the room when she attends the group will help her feel a little safer, reduce her anxiety, and make the experience more bearable.

Adrian has also noticed feelings of anger coming up toward her parents for not supporting her. Even though her anger is warranted (her parents are hurting her with their lack of support and the fact that her mother isn't even trying to understand her), Adrian has realized that this emotion is causing her a lot of distress, and it takes a lot of energy to be so angry all the time. It's also causing a lot of tension in the house, and she doesn't want this to continue, so Adrian starts acting opposite: instead of picking fights with her parents, she's trying to be more civil. Instead of rehashing their arguments in her head and going over and over how unfair things are at home, she tries to see things from her parents' perspective (for example, her mother was raised in her religion, and she has no other experiences to help her understand what Adrian is trying to describe to her, so it's hard for her to understand how Adrian feels). This doesn't mean Adrian agrees with her parents or likes what they're doing, but she can understand where they're coming from, which helps reduce her anger with them. She also tries to get her mind off these things by using her crisis survival skills.

By the way, a helpful tip here is that some emotions (such as anger, where you're judging others or a situation, and shame, where you're judging yourself) not only affect your outward actions but also come with judgmental thoughts. So if you're trying to act opposite to your urge with anger or shame, you need to act opposite as well as *think opposite*, or in a nonjudgmental way.

Have a look at the following chart (Linehan 2014) to help you consider how you would use this skill with some of the emotions you might struggle with.

Emotion	Urge	How to Act Opposite
Anger	Lash out, attack someone or something, physically or verbally Judge the person or situation with which you're angry	Be respectful or civil to the other person; if this feels too difficult, gently avoid the person Change judgments to nonjudgmental, accepting thoughts
Sadness	Hide away from others, isolate yourself Stop doing regular activities	Reach out and connect with others Reengage in usual activities
Fear/Anxiety	Avoid whatever is causing the fear/anxiety Escape the situation causing fear/anxiety	Approach the situation or person causing the fear/anxiety Stay in the situation
Guilt	Stop the behavior causing guilt; make repair (apologize)	Continue the behavior; don't apologize or try to make repair in other ways

Shame	Hide away from others, isolate yourself Judge yourself	Reach out to others; connect; share what you're feeling shame about Change self-judgments to nonjudgments; radically accept; self-validate
Love	Seek connection with the person you love; reach out	Avoid connection with the person you love; don't act on the urge to reach out

Looking at this chart, you might be wondering why on earth you might want to act opposite to the emotion of love. Well, have you ever felt love (or lust, or strong like) for someone who doesn't share your feelings? Or maybe for someone who's already in a relationship with someone else? Perhaps you've found yourself in a relationship that you know isn't healthy (the person doesn't treat you with respect, or maybe you don't share the same values), and you don't want to have those strong feelings for the person. These are some times when acting opposite to love will be helpful.

An important point bears repeating here: acting opposite does not mean stuffing emotions. If you're feeling angry with someone, you can still be angry with them even if you act opposite. It's not about pretending to be otherwise or about stuffing the feeling down. Remember that stuffing or avoiding your emotions is not effective; it typically makes things worse and makes it less likely you'll be able to manage your emotions.

A final point is that choosing to acting opposite even one time might be helpful. You may find that acting opposite doesn't make your emotion completely disappear. If that's the case, don't be discouraged; with some emotions, in some situations, you need repetition. In other words, you need to act opposite a number of times before the emotion comes down. Anxiety is a great example. Adrian has had anxiety about being with new people for some time, so attending the LGBTQI+ group only once is probably not going to make her anxiety go away, but over time if she continues to put herself in that same situation, her brain will come to learn that there is no threat, and her anxiety will disappear.

Acting Opposite, Step by Step

I know this is a lot of information to remember, so here is a summary of how to act opposite to your emotion, step by step.

Step 1: Name the emotion you want to change; validate it (accept it, don't judge it).

Step 2: Identify the urge that goes with the emotion; what's the emotion telling you to do?

Step 3: Ask yourself if the emotion fits the facts in this situation (refer to the discussion of emotions in chapter 5 if you're not sure). If the emotion is not justified, go to step 4. If it is justified, ask yourself if acting on the urge will be effective; if yes, follow the urge—don't act opposite!

Step 4: Ask yourself if you want to change the emotion; if you do, then figure out what the opposite action is, and move on to step 5.

Step 5: Do the opposite action and repeat it until the emotion goes down.

Doing the acting opposite to urge worksheet (Van Dijk 2011) will help you put together everything that you've learned about this skill. First, look at Adrian's worksheet, which shows what happened when she felt the emotion of anger with her parents. Adrian acted the opposite to her urge and used the worksheet to record what happened.

Sample Worksheet: Adrian's Acting Opposite to Urge

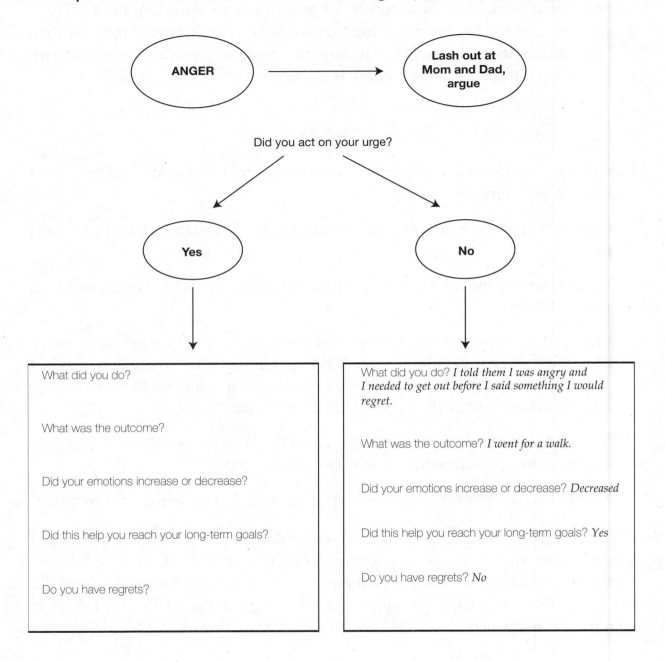

You can use this worksheet to review your own examples of what happens when you feel a strong emotion and an urge that goes with it. Visit http://www.newhar binger.com/45458 to download copies of this worksheet.

Worksheet: Acting Opposite to Urge

The next time you experience a strong emotion that goes with an urge, afterward record what happened, whether you acted on the urge or you acted opposite to it. Write down the emotion and the urge, and whether or not you acted on the urge, and then answer the questions that follow.

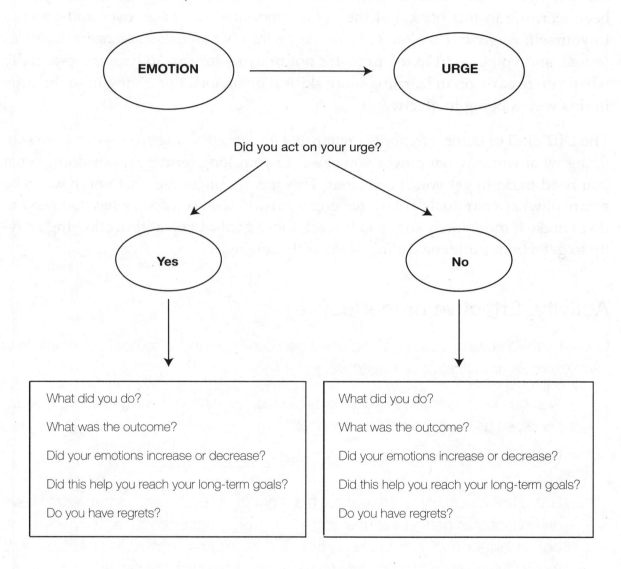

Did you act on your urge?

What did you do?	What did you do?
What was the outcome?	What was the outcome?
Did your emotions increase or decrease?	Did your emotions increase or decrease?
Did this help you reach your long-term goals?	Did this help you reach your long-term goals?
Do you have regrets?	Do you have regrets?

Now that you've learned about being willing and how to use the skill of acting opposite when you're experiencing a strong emotion, it will help to look at the more general skill of how to be effective.

Being Effective

Do you notice that you often act from your emotional self, doing what feels *good* or *right*, rather than doing what would be skillful, or what's helpful or healthy for you in the long term? For example, if you have an urge to engage in your target behavior, you might notice thoughts about trying to use some of the skills you've been learning in this book, but then your emotional self takes over and you say to yourself, *Forget it, I don't feel like working hard right now. It's just easier to do this instead*, and you give in to the urge. It's not unusual for this to happen, especially when you're early on in learning more skillful behaviors. But giving in to the urge in this way is being ineffective.

The DBT skill of being *effective* (Linehan 1993) is about acting from your wise self: doing what works, what moves you closer to your long-term goals, or doing what you need to do to get your needs met. This means, of course, that you have to be aware of what your goals are in the long term and then consider what you need to do to make it more likely that you'll reach those goals. Look at the following activity to get a better understanding of what this means.

Activity: Effective or Ineffective?

Consider the following situations and see if you can figure out whether the behaviors in each example are effective or ineffective.

1. Alex has been wanting to get a part-time job, but when he finally got an interview, he felt so anxious, he called to cancel it.

   Was his behavior effective or ineffective? _____

2. Shelly knows she needs to get her math grade up by the end of the year to have any chance of getting into the engineering program she wants. But when she got an invitation to go to a big party, she couldn't bring herself to say no, so she went anyway, even though she knew she needed that time to study for her exam.

   Was her behavior effective or ineffective? _____

3. Jamie's parents had finally agreed that if he saved enough money, they would help him buy a car. Because this was his number one goal, he jumped at the chance to work overtime on the long weekend, even though it meant he had to cancel his camping trip.

Was his behavior effective or ineffective? _____

4. Janice knows she tends to push people away because she lashes out at them in anger. When her friend Sharon said something that she found hurtful, she managed to keep her immediate reaction to herself, took some time to think about it, and was later able to tell Sharon about her hurt feelings. Sharon was able to clarify what she meant, and Janice felt good about herself for how she handled this situation.

Was her behavior effective or ineffective? _____

5. Rene felt like his parents didn't understand how much his depression and anxiety limited his ability to do things, and they were constantly getting on his case to help out around the house. He wanted to reduce the number of arguments they were having, because arguing stressed him out more, so he was pushing himself to tell them when he was really struggling with his feelings and was also keeping his bedroom clean like they were asking him to.

Was his behavior effective or ineffective? _____

Answer key: 1. Ineffective. 2. Ineffective. 3. Effective. 4. Effective. 5. Effective.

Now that you're hopefully getting a better idea of what it means to be effective and ineffective, you can start looking at how to use this skill in your own life.

Activity: How Can You Be More Effective?

First, think of a time when you were ineffective, when you acted in a way that may have brought you some sort of short-term satisfaction, but in the long run, your behavior wasn't moving you in the direction of your goals. Make some notes about the situation here:

_____

_____

_____

In order to be effective, you have to be aware of what your long-term goals are. What is it that you're trying to accomplish in the long run? Take a minute now and consider some goals you have generally in your life, or in a specific situation you're currently struggling with, and make some notes here:

_____

_____

_____

Once you decide on this, your next step is to think about what you can do that will make it more likely that you'll reach those goals. Keep in mind that acting effectively (or using any other DBT skill) doesn't guarantee that you'll get what you want in a situation. But if you're acting skillfully—for example, using crisis survival skills to eliminate your target behaviors, and using mindfulness, being nonjudgmental, self-validation, and reality acceptance to manage emotions in healthier ways—it makes sense that your chances of reaching your goal will increase. See if you can come up with some skills that would help you move in the direction of reaching those goals, and make some notes here:

_____

_____

_____

Finally, write down your thoughts about what might be getting in your way of reaching those goals:

_____

_____

_____

_____

What Gets in the Way?

One thing that often gets in the way of being effective is our thoughts about the situation: we tend to react to how we think a situation *should* be rather than responding to reality as it really is (Linehan 1993). Think of a time, for example, when you've thought to yourself that something wasn't *fair*, or *should* or *shouldn't* be a certain way. If you think it's not fair that your curfew is 10:00 p.m., it might influence your decision to stay out until 11:00 p.m. instead, but staying out that late isn't effective if your long-term goal is to be treated like an adult by your parents. Or if you have the thought that you shouldn't have to tell your best friend how you feel, and this stops you from communicating your feelings to them, you're likely not working toward your long-term goal of having a healthy relationship with this person. It can be helpful if you ask yourself, *Is it more important that I be right, or that I get what I want?* (Linehan 2005).

Here's a reminder of some of the other skills you've already read about in this book that can help you be more effective:

- Go stick your face in cold water or do a forward bend to help you reduce the intensity of your emotion and get to your wise self.

- Take an open posture and put on a half smile to help you be more willing to do what's effective.

- Practice radically accepting that things are as they are.

- Take a nonjudgmental stance toward others, the situation, and yourself.

Wrapping Up

In this chapter, you've learned about the skill of acting opposite to your emotion, which will help you reduce the intensity of your emotion. Remember that when the feelings are less intense, they'll be more manageable and less likely to lead to you engaging in those target behaviors. You've also learned about willingness and willfulness, what it means to be effective, and some strategies to help you implement these skills in your life.

The most healthy and helpful balance we need to strike in our lives, however, is to accept things as they are (our emotions, thoughts, behaviors, and so on), and then if we don't like how things are, we can look to see if there's something we can do to change it. As you continue to work through this book, let that theme guide you: accept it—reality, your feelings, yourself—and then see whether you can do something to make it different if you don't want it to be that way. In the next chapter, you'll apply these and other skills in your relationships. I hope you're hanging in there, practicing skills, and feeling willing to continue to learn. I know it's hard, but remember to be effective: keep your long-term goals in mind!

Chapter 8

The Importance of Relationships

Relationships can bring us love, companionship, and support, they can bring us joy and fulfillment, and they can also be really complicated and a huge source of emotional pain. But, like it or not, relationships are necessary for our survival. This means that we need social support, intimacy, and connection with others to thrive. In fact, research has shown that loneliness—the emotion that results from a lack of these connections—can lead to various psychiatric disorders and physical health problems. One study (Holt-Lunstad et al. 2015) found that a lack of social connections carried health risks similar to smoking up to fifteen cigarettes a day!

In this chapter, I'm going to ask you to look more closely at your relationships—with your parents, friends, teachers, coaches, coworkers, classmates, and whoever else you have in your life—to see how much (or how little) of your emotional pain and resulting target behaviors are related to them. You'll be looking at some skills to help you navigate these relationships in healthier ways, so you'll be more effective in communicating with others and in making wise choices with friends and other people you know; at times, this might include making the difficult decision to end a relationship. To begin, read Leona's story and notice how problems in one particular relationship contributed to her target behavior.

Leona's Story

Leona and Lilian had been friends since first grade. Leona enjoyed spending time with Lilian, but over the last couple of years, their relationship had become more stressful, as Leona started to notice more and more that they had developed very different values, which was sometimes leading to disagreements. Lilian, for example, was not shy about the fact that she enjoyed having sex and would quite often hook up with people at parties they went to. Leona, on the other hand, didn't like the idea of having sex outside of a relationship, because it didn't reflect her values. She found that Lilian also put pressure on her to do things she wasn't comfortable with, and this really bothered her, because she believed that everyone should be free to make their own choices for themselves, from their wise self.

Leona tried to talk to Lilian about some of these problems, but Lilian would make light of Leona's concerns and tease her for being a buzzkill. Sometimes this would end in the two of them fighting, and more than once, this had contributed to Leona's feeling so anxious and angry at both herself and Lilian that she ended up cutting. When she and Lilian were together, Leona would sometimes end up doing things that went against her morals and values, which would cause feelings of guilt and shame, and this ended in her cutting more than once. Leona knew she had to do something about this relationship to get to a healthier place for herself, but she didn't have any other close friends, so the idea of no longer having Lilian was scary for her.

Leona was very aware that her lack of other friendships was a problem, especially once she recognized that she needed to take steps to do something about the relationship that had turned unhealthy with Lilian. This is the kind of awareness we all need so that we can work to make changes in our lives when necessary.

The next activity will increase your awareness of what's happening with relationships in your own life.

Activity: Whom Do You Have in Your Life?

Answer the following questions to help you consider who offers you support and friendship. Do your best to not judge whatever comes up, and don't worry about whether you've put people in the right category, but just think about who is in your life, and write the names down where they fit for you.

1. **Family support.** Are there any particular family members with whom you're close? This might be a parent or a sibling, aunt or uncle, grandparent, or cousin. Don't write all your family members in the blanks, but take care to add only the

names of those who are supportive. Think about who listens to you. Who understands you? Can you count on them when things are difficult?

_____   _____   _____

_____   _____   _____

2. **Supportive friends.** Think about the friends you have in your life who are there when you need them. These are people you're comfortable sharing at least some of your secrets and problems with. They are the friends you can rely on when you're struggling.

_____   _____   _____

_____   _____   _____

3. **Social friends.** There are different levels of friendship, and social friends are people with whom you enjoy spending time, maybe going to the movies or doing certain other activities with, but they're not people with whom you share a lot of your personal stuff. They're fun to hang out with, but you don't tell them your secrets.

_____   _____   _____

_____   _____   _____

4. **Role models and mentors.** Do you have people in your life whom you look up to? Anyone you consider a healthy, positive role model? A person you respect and by whom you feel respected in return? Examples here might be a teacher, guidance counselor, or coach (past or present). It could be someone at your church, your boss or someone you know at work, or a professional, like your family doctor or a therapist you're seeing or have seen in the past.

_____   _____   _____

_____   _____   _____

5. **Unhealthy relationships.** Finally, are there relationships that you consider to be unhealthy in some way? Maybe you know that when you get together with a

particular friend, you tend to make unwise choices for yourself, or you feel pressure to act in ways that go against your morals and values (like Leona with Lilian), or maybe it's difficult for you to see your friend make choices that you think are unwise or unhealthy. Another example might be a relationship that feels one-sided, where you do more of the giving than the taking. Whatever the case, carefully consider if you have any unhealthy or unsatisfying relationships, relationships that feel out of balance in some way, and write the names of those people here.

_____ _____ _____

_____ _____ _____

Take a moment now to reflect on what this exercise was like for you. Was it difficult? Are you judging? (You might have the thought *This is awful. I should have more people. What's wrong with me?*) Are certain emotions coming up as you look at what you've written? Looking at the people you've listed in this activity, do you have any thoughts about changes you need to make, whether it's increasing the number of people in certain areas of your life or perhaps working on improving—or even ending—certain unhealthy relationships? Jot down your thoughts here.

_____

_____

_____

_____

_____

What to Do About Unhealthy Relationships

Like Leona, you may have realized that you have an unhealthy relationship—or more than one!—that you need to do something about, so let's look at what your options are for this.

Make a Wise Choice

First, it's important that you make the choice from your wise self whether to keep or end the relationship. It can be easy to get to a point of feeling so fed up or frustrated with someone that ending the relationship feels like the best thing to do, but it's not a good idea for this decision to be based on your emotions. You can use the pros and cons chart from chapter 1 to help you make a balanced decision.

Pros of Ending the Relationship	Cons of Ending the Relationship
Pros of Not Ending the Relationship	Cons of Not Ending the Relationship

By examining the pros and cons, and by continuing to practice the strategies you learned in chapter 4 to help you get to that place of internal wisdom, over time you'll feel more confident about your ability to make healthier choices like these for yourself.

Safety First!

Remember that everyone has the right to be physically and emotionally safe and respected, so if you're in a relationship (romantic, friendship, or with a family member) where you are being abused in any way, please ask someone you trust for help. If you're not sure whether what you're experiencing is abuse, you still need to talk to someone about it. It's not uncommon for people in these kinds of situations to think the word "abuse" is too strong, so you might need an outside perspective to help you get to your wise self. Whatever you do, please keep yourself safe.

If the relationship isn't abusive, unsafe, or damaging to you, you might decide to keep the relationship, in which case you need to do some work on it so the relationship is healthier and more satisfying. Whether you decide to end the relationship or keep it and work on it, you'll need to develop the communication skills covered a little later in this chapter. But before going there, let's look at what your options are when you know you need to increase the number of people in your life.

Increasing Relationships in Your Life

If, like Leona, you realize that you don't have enough healthy relationships in your life, I hope you see the importance of increasing your connections with others. Loneliness is life threatening! It can be hard to make this decision, especially when you've had a history of being bullied, for example, or if you have social anxiety where your fear holds you back from connecting with others. So again, do your best to get to your wise self to make a decision about this, recognizing that you may not get to the point of really wanting to do this but you know (from your wise self) that it's what you need to do. Once you get to this point, here's a series of activities to help you work on increasing the number of relationships you have in your life right now. Keeping in mind that this might be scary, do your best to brainstorm here. There's no need to put any of these plans into action yet.

Activity: Reconnecting

First, think about people from your past: do you have anyone with whom you would want to reconnect? They may be someone who went to your school or played the same sport as you or belonged to the same club but you're no longer in touch with them, for whatever reason. Write down the names of any people who come to mind:

_____

_____

Now choose one of these people; it might be someone who would be easy to find or who would be likely to respond if you reached out. Now consider how you might get in touch with that person. This might not be a problem if they still go to your school or if your parents are friends with their parents; maybe you still have their phone number and you can send them a text; or maybe you're still connected on Instagram and you can send them a message there. Whatever the case, write down some thoughts about how you could get in touch.

_____

_____

Now think about what you would say when you reach out to this person. It might be as straightforward as sending a text or a Snapchat. But maybe you had a falling-out with them and you need to clear the air or perhaps apologize for something that happened between the two of you—for example, maybe you were struggling to manage your emotions back then, and this person got frustrated with being the target of your anger, in which case you can explain to them that you're working on this and you've realized you owe them an apology. Or perhaps your anxiety was out of control back then, and you kept canceling plans at the last minute because your anxiety kept getting in the way. Think about what that first conversation might look like and write your thoughts down here.

_____

_____

_____

_____

Last, of course, comes the hard part—putting yourself out there. When you're ready, put your plan into action, using some of your other skills to help you. For example, be mindful, doing your best to not catastrophize about the response you might get; act opposite to the anxiety that might be coming up, and push yourself to reach out in spite of the fear. Keep in mind that the relationship won't be the same as it was before—things are always changing!—and that connections take time to develop, so have patience and pat yourself on the back for taking the risk. I hope it pays off for you!

Activity: Deepening Current Connections

The second option for increasing the people in your life is to think about who you currently have in your life with whom you might be interested in developing a deeper connection. Maybe there's a new student in your English class, or someone who's on the same sports team or attends the same club, who is someone you'd like to get to know better. If you have a job or do volunteer work, look around to see if there's someone there you'd be interested in getting to know better. Write down any names that come to mind here.

_____

_____

Now think about how you can start to develop this friendship, such as inviting the new kid to sit with you at lunch or striking up a conversation with someone at work, instead of keeping to yourself. Jot your ideas down here:

_____

_____

Again, the hard part comes next, when you have to start putting the plan into place. Remember that this is something you need to do for your emotional and physical health and that this decision is coming from your wise self. The more you push yourself outside of your comfort zone, the more effective you'll feel as you work toward your goals, even if there are times when you don't get the results you were hoping for.

Activity: Creating New Opportunities

This can be hard to do, but if reconnecting or if deepening your connections isn't an option, then you will have to work instead on creating new opportunities to meet people who might turn into friends. You could start playing a new sport, head over to the library to study instead of staying at home, or find a part-time job or volunteer work. Brainstorm and write your ideas here.

_____

_____

_____

_____

While it's probably scary to think of going out and meeting new people in this way, remember that relationships are necessary. Having more relationships in your life will help you feel better about yourself, as you recognize that you are deserving of the love and respect of others—and of yourself—and this will help you eliminate your target behavior. Are there things you can do to make taking this step any easier? For example, do you have someone who could go with you to the club after school that you're thinking of joining, at least the first time? Maybe you know someone who already does volunteer work at the food bank or animal shelter and you can go with them. Or perhaps you know someone else in a similar situation, and you can work on increasing relationships together, being there to support one another.

Now that you're working on increasing the people in your life, the next step is looking at how you can create healthy relationships with these people and keep these relationships balanced and satisfying.

Healthy Communication

Many of us struggle to communicate in healthy ways. Sometimes this is because emotions get in the way. We may be afraid of how others will respond if we try to get our needs met. We might not think we deserve to get what we want. We might judge ourselves as selfish and feel ashamed for trying to get something from someone. Sometimes it's because we aren't self-aware, and we haven't recognized that we have unmet needs or wants. And sometimes we simply don't know how to ask effectively for things from others. Regardless of where the struggle comes from, the end result is the same: it creates extra emotional pain, which will make it more likely that you turn back to those self-harming and self-destructive behaviors.

So the first question to start asking yourself is, *What's getting in the way?* Here, of course, some of the skills you've already learned will be helpful: mindfulness (from chapter 3) will help you tune into this a little more; when you can access your wise self (from chapter 4), you'll be more able to identify what the problem is without judging it, and you'll be more able to take steps—such as asking someone for help—to figure out what the problem is. Mindfulness and accessing your internal wisdom will also help you figure out what emotions might be getting in the way of acting more skillfully, so you can start doing something to reduce the intensity of the emotion, like using the skill of acting opposite (from chapter 7), or reducing your vulnerability to your emotions through lifestyles changes, like balancing your sleep (from chapter 4).

It's also not at all uncommon for people to have problematic thoughts or beliefs about relationships and communicating. The next activity will help you figure out if you have thoughts or beliefs that might be getting in your way.

Activity: Faulty Beliefs About Relationships

Consider each of the following untrue statements about relationships, and ask yourself if you believe any of them. It could be only a part of you that does—maybe it's your emotional self! In each case, see if you can come up with a way of challenging—or talking back to—these faulty beliefs. Here are a couple of examples:

Thought: *It's selfish to ask others for things.*

Challenge: *Letting others know what I want will keep my relationships healthy in the long run.*

Thought: *I should always put others first.*

Challenge: *Sometimes I can choose to put others first, but I also have to put my own needs first sometimes.*

Now it's your turn. Challenge the following thoughts.

1. **Thought:** *I won't be able to handle it if someone gets angry with me.*

   Challenge: _____

2. **Thought:** *Asking for help means I'm weak.*

   Challenge: _____

3. **Thought:** *I shouldn't have to ask for things from the people I'm close to, because they should know what I need.*

   Challenge: _____

4. **Thought:** *If others aren't willing to do more for me, clearly they don't care about me.*

   Challenge: _____

5. **Thought:** *Saying no to someone is wrong.*

   Challenge: _____

6. **Thought:** *It's selfish if I put my own needs before others' needs.*

   Challenge: _____

7. **Thought:** *I don't need friends in my life.*

   Challenge: _____

8. **Thought:** *I must really be stupid if I can't do this myself.*

   Challenge: _____

Possible answers:

1. *I don't like it when others get angry with me, but it's not the end of the world.*

2. *Everyone needs help sometimes, and it takes strength to ask for it.*

3. *No one is a mind reader, so sometimes I need to tell others what I want or need.*

4. *Everyone has to decide for themselves what they're willing and able to do for others; how much they do or don't do for me is no indicator of how much they care.*

5. *It's okay to say no to others sometimes, just like they'll say no to me at times.*

6. *I'm allowed to choose when to put others' needs first and when to put my own needs first.*

7. *Everyone needs friends and support.*

8. *No one can do everything on their own; it doesn't mean anything about me as a person if I need help from others.*

Now see if you can think of some faulty beliefs that get in your way in relationships, and challenge those thoughts. If you have difficulty with this, ask someone you trust for help.

Thought: _____

Challenge: _____

Thought: _____

Challenge: _____

If you see that faulty beliefs about relationships are getting in your way, the next step is to work on changing them. Again, practice will help. Just noticing when these problematic beliefs pop up, and talking back to them by reading the challenging statements to yourself, will help you change that internal chatter. Here are a couple of tips: see if you can get to your wise self with these thoughts, taking a more balanced and nonjudgmental perspective. You can also try the trick of considering what you would say to someone you care about if they expressed these things: for example, if your best friend or your little sister told you she believed she should always put others' needs before her own, what would you say to her?

Remember that changing thoughts takes time, so this is just the first step. The good news is, you can work on changing your behavior at the same time, and this will help change the way you think about things. Next come some skills to help you start communicating in healthier ways.

How to Communicate Assertively

Being assertive means expressing your emotions, thoughts, and beliefs in a clear way and in a way that is respectful both to yourself and to the person you're communicating with. It involves caring about the other person and their needs, which means that negotiation and compromise often come into play, as you try to meet your own needs as well as those of the other person.

Many people struggle to be assertive because they don't feel they deserve to ask for things from others. If you don't feel good about yourself, you might struggle to tell people how you really feel, what your opinion is, and so on. The good news is that the more you assert yourself, the better you'll feel about yourself over time, so being assertive can actually help improve not just your relationships but also your self-esteem. And, of course, the healthier your relationships are and the better you feel about yourself, the less you'll want to turn to those target behaviors you've been using to cope.

BE CLEAR ABOUT YOUR GOALS

The first step in assertiveness is getting clear on what you want. If you don't know what your goal is in a situation, how can you expect to communicate it to the other person? Think back to Leona as an example. She knows that she wants her relationship with Lilian to change, but what does she want to be different? Does she want to end the relationship altogether? Possibly take a break? Or maybe keep the relationship and try to improve it, so it's no longer contributing to her painful emotions and self-harming behavior? Leona isn't going to be able to effectively communicate this to Lilian until she's clear on it herself. Once she has that clarity, she can start to assertively ask Lilian for what she wants. Of course, figuring out what you want can be challenging, so here are some ideas for you to consider:

- Doing a pros and cons chart will certainly help you access your wise self to get some clarity around your goals.

- Being mindfully aware of your thoughts and emotions when you're spending time with your friend will help you better understand what your values are (from chapter 3).

- Being nonjudgmental, accepting, and validating yourself will improve your self-respect and self-esteem, allowing you to see more clearly what would be healthy for you (see chapter 6).

- Developing friendships with others will improve your self-confidence and increase your willingness to work toward changing unhealthy relationships.

The next step, once you know what you want in your relationship, is to use these DBT skills to be more assertive (Linehan 1993).

DESCRIBE THE SITUATION

When you're being assertive, it's best to begin by describing the situation you want to discuss with the other person, sticking to the facts of the situation, and staying away from judgments and blaming. Essentially, you're describing for the other person what this conversation is going to be about.

STATE YOUR OPINION AND EMOTIONS

Next you express your opinions and your feelings (again, not judging, and not blaming!) about the situation you've just described.

CLEARLY STATE WHAT YOU WANT

This is where you get very specific about what you're asking for. Be sure to make a clear request. Too often, we expect others to read our mind about what we'd like. For example, if it's your turn to do the dishes and you say to your parents, "There are a ton of dishes tonight and it's late," you may want them to help you do the dishes, or you may want them to say it's okay to leave the dishes until tomorrow. But your parents aren't mind readers, so it's important to be clear, "Could you give me a hand with the dishes?" or "Would it be okay to leave them for tomorrow?"

REINFORCE

It can be helpful if you tell the other person what they're going to get out of giving you what you're asking for. For example, if you approached your sister for help with the dishes, you could let her know that if she helps you tonight, you'll help her tomorrow night when it's her turn. This way, the other person will be more likely to want to help, because they see that it's not just all about you and that you're willing to compromise.

Leona used these skills to communicate assertively after she decided that she wants to take a break from her relationship with Lilian for some time. Here's what she said.

Describe: *We've been friends for a very long time.*

State opinions and emotions: *I value your friendship, and I don't want to lose that. As you know, I've recently been struggling more with managing my emotions. I've been noticing lately that we've grown apart in terms of who we are, our values, and what we enjoy doing, and this has been adding to my feelings of sadness and anxiety. Because of this, I think it would be helpful for me to take a step back to evaluate my decision making and to get a handle on my emotions.*

State what you want: *I want to take a break from our friendship, with no contact of any kind, for three months.*

Reinforce: *I'd really appreciate it if you would give me this space with no contact. This will give me time to focus on getting healthier, which will also allow me to be a better friend to you.*

You can imagine how difficult it would be for Leona to have this conversation with Lilian, and chances are that Lilian is going to be hurt by Leona's request. But keep in mind that when communicating assertively, you are being respectful to both yourself and the other person, which means that, even if Lilian is hurt, Leona hasn't done anything on purpose to hurt her (such as blaming or judging). This is one of those times where Leona made a wise decision to put her own needs before those of her friend. Having said that, there are some additional skills that might help her to be effective in this situation, which I'll talk about in the next section.

First, do you have something that you want from someone but you haven't figured out how to ask for it? Or perhaps someone has asked you for something, and you're not sure how to say no. Assertiveness will help in either scenario.

Activity: Be Assertive

In the space provided, write some notes about how to make your request or say no to another person using these skills.

1. Describe: _____

_____

2. State opinions and emotions: _____

_____

3. State what you want: _____

_____

4. Reinforce: _____

_____

Using these strategies will make it more likely that you'll get your needs met, keep a good relationship with the person, and feel good about yourself after the conversation. And this, of course, is a recipe for reducing your target behavior, as you'll likely feel good about the outcome. Here are a few more skills that will help you to be assertive.

Additional Skills for Assertiveness

These skills will both help you get what you want and make it more likely that you'll keep a good connection with the other person and feel good about yourself when the conversation is over.

LISTEN MINDFULLY, BE INTERESTED, AND VALIDATE

It will go a long way if the other person feels that you're really paying attention and are genuinely interested in what they have to say, so eliminate potential distractions. Put away your phone, shut your laptop, make eye contact, and really focus on the other person. Ask questions and be interested in the other person's responses.

Validating others also goes a long way toward maintaining or even improving relationships. Remember the skill of self-validation that we talked about in chapter 6? Accepting your emotions as they are, right? Well, validating the other person works similarly. Ask questions to clarify, and even repeat back to the person what they've said to you, to let them know that you're listening and understand. Let the person know that what they have to say is important to you and that you accept it, even if you don't agree with it or like it. Think of a time when someone has responded this way to you and how good it felt to know the other person understood or accepted you; doing the same for the people in your life will go a long way toward improving your relationships.

BE GENUINE AND USE HUMOR

Assertiveness isn't synonymous with serious! So when appropriate, try to lighten the mood by smiling, laughing, and using humor. Doing your best to be light-hearted in the interaction when you can, even if it's a serious conversation, can help reduce tension, soothe emotions, and improve the likelihood of a positive outcome.

STICK TO YOUR VALUES

You did some work in chapter 3 to figure out what your values are. Now that you have a better understanding of your values, you'll be more able to stick to them when you're being assertive. Ask yourself how you would like to be treated by others: you probably wouldn't want to be judged, blamed, yelled at, called names, and so on. So treat the other person the way you would like to be treated. Consider what you can do to encourage this person to help you. Finally, imagine you have an audience for this interaction: if people you respect were watching you, would you be embarrassed or ashamed, or would you feel comfortable continuing to behave the way you are?

These are the skills to help you communicate more effectively with others, but this is only one set of skills you can use to create healthy and satisfying relationships. There are a few more skills to use with this goal in mind.

How to Train Your People

You might recall from chapter 1 that all animals—human beings included—learn the same way: we do more of what we're rewarded for and less of what we're not rewarded—or what we're punished—for. By applying this knowledge, you can get to a healthier place with the people in your life and get more of what you want (and less of what you don't want!) in your relationships.

Rewarding Others

When someone does something you would like more of in the future, you need to find a way to reward them. For example, if your little sister helps you with the dishes, and you say a big thank you, and maybe give her a hug or do something nice for her in return, it's a reward for her helping behavior. When you do this, you'll be more likely to get more of that helpful behavior from her in the future. On the other hand, if you're doing the dishes together and you start arguing with each other—assuming your sister doesn't like to argue and this is a negative (punishing) experience—you'll be less likely to get that helping behavior from her in the future.

Again, we all learn this way. Think of some times when you've been on the receiving end of these rewards or punishments: maybe you got an A+ on a paper you had put a lot of effort into; that A+ is the reward that will make it more likely you'll work hard again in the future—although this might also be an example of how there are no guarantees here! When Mr. Smith caught you using your cell phone in class and you got detention, that punishment likely made it more likely you'll think twice the next time you have an urge to text in Mr. Smith's class—or at least more likely you'll learn how to hide it better! Using some of these principles can help you be more effective in getting what you want in life. It's also true that rewards, or reinforcers, tend to be more effective than punishments. Of course, you can't control how others behave, but using these skills, you can sometimes have an influence on their behaviors.

Activity: Influencing Behaviors in Others

See if you can come up with some ideas for how the people in these scenarios can get what they want by influencing another's behavior. Write your ideas in the space provided. Some suggestions appear at the end of the exercise.

1. Carly's BFF knows that Carly likes to get to bed early because she's up early in the morning for volleyball practice. Carly has asked her BFF not to call after 10:00 p.m., but her BFF continues to call late at night anyway and she ends up not getting enough sleep. How can Carly make it more likely she'll get what she wants?

    _____

    _____

    _____

2. Michael's older brother sometimes gives him a ride to school when he's in a good mood. How can Michael get rides to school more often?

    _____

    _____

    _____

3. Jessica's significant other has a habit that annoys her: when they're supposed to be spending time with Jessica, they're on their phone most of the time texting or Googling. They insist they're still paying attention to Jessica, but she's not feeling it, and she's used her assertiveness skills to let them know she'd like them to work on changing this behavior. How can she get more of her significant other's undivided attention when the two of them are together?

    _____

    _____

    _____

4. Braden has noticed that his boss tends to be unclear when he's leaving instructions for what he'd like done in his absence. Braden has communicated this to him, and it seems that his boss has tried to make changes, but he's still inconsistent. What can Braden do to make it more likely his boss will continue to work on this and get more consistent in communicating his expectations?

_____

_____

_____

5. Brittany is frustrated with her parents' rules and feels like they don't trust her. She's sixteen and her curfew is still 10:00 p.m., unlike most of her friends who are allowed to stay out at least until midnight on weekends. She's gotten her parents to agree to 11:00 p.m. sometimes, but she wants more leeway. How might she be more likely to get more of this freedom from her parents?

_____

_____

_____

Possible answers:

1. When her BFF calls before 10:00 p.m., Carly can thank them for being aware of the time and calling early enough so she can spend some time talking to them. Then she can make sure she spends quality time talking to them and being mindful in the interaction.

2. Michael can thank his brother when he does drive him; he might point out that it's nice to spend some extra time with him. While they're driving in together, Michael might be able to think of something to make the car ride more enjoyable for his brother: asking his brother about his sports team, favorite class, or particular interest so that his brother gets to spend time talking about something he enjoys. Michael could also offer him something in return for driving. Some gas money? Washing his car in the driveway? Taking his brother's turn doing a chore he doesn't like?

3. When her significant other is paying attention in the way she wants, Jessica can make sure she's giving her undivided attention in return; she can point out that when her significant other puts the phone aside, this makes a difference for their time together, and she can communicate the pleasurable feelings that come up for her knowing that she's important enough for her significant other to work on taking her request seriously.

4. Braden can point out to his boss the positive consequences of when his boss has been clearer with his instructions: noting how his boss is going to benefit more as people are more able to give him what he's looking for, and perhaps pointing out the benefit to morale or other positives Braden sees resulting from this change in behavior.

5. Brittany can make sure she sticks to her parents' curfew, which will show them that she is responsible and that she respects their wishes, making it more likely she'll get more of what she's looking for. A thank-you will also go a long way here, and maybe Brittany can figure out something else that would be reinforcing for her parents. For example, if they let her stay out an extra hour, she could offer to drive her sibling to swimming lessons this week.

Now think about your own life: what do you want others to be doing more of, and how can you get that? Are there things that others are doing that you'd like them to change? Think about how you can communicate your wishes to them assertively, and then consider what you can do to make it more likely they'll give you more of what you're looking for and less of what you don't want. Make some notes here:

_____

_____

_____

_____

_____

Wrapping Up

You've learned a lot of skills in this chapter that will help with relationships. Relationships will have a big influence on your mood and how you feel about yourself, which is why it's so important that you have enough relationships in your life and that these relationships are healthy and satisfying for you. If you don't have enough people in your life, you can begin to consider what you might be willing to do about it. If you have unhealthy relationships, you can start to think about steps to take to either improve those relationships or perhaps end them. And finally, you've learned a lot of skills that will help you start new relationships off on the right footing and that will improve or keep healthy the relationships you already have in your life. When you have healthy relationships, you'll be less likely to want to engage in those target behaviors. You'll have support from others to help you act in healthier ways, and you may even come to see yourself through the eyes of the people who care about you and that you deserve to take better care of yourself!

As this book draws to a close, I'd like you to take the opportunity to think about where you are now with your target behavior and the skills you've been learning and where you'd like to go. I'll review strategies in the conclusion to help you stay on this path that you've started down toward a healthier life. So, hang in there, and when you're ready, turn the page.

Conclusion

Where Are You Now?

You did it! You've made it to the end of the book. First, congratulations for staying with it to learn all of the skills this book had to offer; and second, please don't get frustrated if you haven't completely eliminated your problem behavior, or if you don't feel "happy," or if all of the problems in your life haven't miraculously disappeared. Remember that these skills do not get rid of pain (or create a life of pure happiness, since no one is happy all the time!), nor do they make problems go away. Building a life worth living takes time and a lot of energy and effort! It's an ongoing process. The good news is, you've started yourself on this path.

I want to review some of the most important skills to help you to stay on this path and continue to make improvements: the pros and cons chart, writing a letter to yourself, and willingness.

Reviewing Your Pros and Cons Chart

To start with, it's a good idea to go back to the pros and cons you did in chapter 1. Take a good look at what you've written there and see if you have any changes to make, now that you've learned more about your target behavior and some skills to help you work on eliminating it. The chart may stay the same, and that's okay, but your perspective may have shifted, and you might have additions or deletions to make, or you might find that the weight of some of those responses has changed, if you used the 1 to 3 rating scale.

If you haven't been using skills to change your behavior, now would be a good time to do a new pros and cons chart on using skills.

Pros of Using Skills	Cons of Using Skills
Pros of Not Using Skills	Cons of Not Using Skills

One last note here. Many people who do self-harming or self-destructive behaviors have more than one unhealthy behavior they use in their attempts to manage their emotions. If this is the case for you, and if you have been using skills and managed to eliminate the target behavior you started with, you can now start looking at how to work on another target behavior. Again, though, do not rush with this. Giving yourself some time to adjust to your new reality—and not trying to take on everything at once—will make it more likely that you'll see positive changes in the long run.

Writing a Letter to Your Self

As you learned in chapter 2, writing a letter to your unwell self is a skill that can help you get through the crisis without making things worse. But you can also write a letter to yourself to motivate you to keep working hard to not fall back into those self-harming and self-destructive behaviors. So from the perspective of your wise self, perhaps when you're able to see some progress you've made—maybe even able to feel a bit of pride in yourself for starting to make changes—start writing some notes to yourself about what's different in your life. The next activity will help you with this.

Activity: Self-Assessment

Do this self-assessment to consider what might go into a letter to yourself. If your answers to any of these questions are negative or discouraging—or you don't like your answer for some reason—that's okay. Answer the question honestly, accept that this is the reality, and then move on to the next question.

1. In chapter 1, you set a goal for yourself. Fill in the blanks here with your original responses:

    My goal for myself has been to (circle one):

    STOP   REDUCE   OTHER: _____

    the following behavior(s): _____

    Now, think about what you've done over the period of time you've been working through this book. Have you reached your goal? Eliminated the problem behavior? Reduced it? Learned more about it? Make some notes here:

    _____

    _____

    _____

    _____

2. If you've reduced or eliminated your behavior, how does that make you feel? What are your thoughts about it?

    _____

    _____

3. What are your thoughts and feelings when you're able to delay acting on the urge by even fifteen minutes?

    _____

    _____

4. Have you seen changes in different areas of your life as a result of reducing or eliminating your self-harming or self-destructive behavior? Changes in relationships, feelings about yourself, self-judgments? Jot some notes about this:

    _____

    _____

    _____

5. Have other people made positive comments on any changes they've seen in you, even if you haven't seen them yourself? If so, write the comments here:

    _____

    _____

6. Have you learned anything about yourself in doing this work? Answer this question even if you haven't seen any changes in your behavior just yet. Perhaps you've discovered what some of your values are or what would make your life more worth living, envisioning a future career, relationships, goals for school, and so on.

    _____

    _____

    _____

7. In working through this book, have you found a skill (or several) that particularly resonated with you, that you've found especially helpful or beneficial? Even if you haven't been able to use the skill (or skills) yet, perhaps you can see how helpful it will be once you're more able to bring it into your life. Jot any thoughts about this here:

    _____

    _____

    _____

Put all of this together now. In the space provided, write a letter from your wise, possibly even healthier self, to your unwell self, that is, your emotion-minded self who wants to continue with or go back to that self-harming or self-destructive behavior. What does that unhealthy self need to know? How can you encourage that emotional self to help you not act on the urges when they arise?

_____

_____

_____

_____

_____

_____

_____

_____

_____

_____

_____

_____

_____

_____

_____

_____

_____

Once you've written this letter to yourself, the next step is to figure out where to put it. My suggestion would be to put it somewhere you'll be able to see it: you might put it in your phone or tablet, so you always have it with you; if privacy isn't an issue, you might decide to write it out for yourself and hang it on your wall or even frame it. Whatever you do with this letter, make sure you add it to your list of crisis survival skills (from chapter 2)! It's important to read this letter to yourself not just when you're starting to get into crisis or notice that urge but also whenever you want a reminder of the positive changes you've made and are continuing to strive toward.

On that note, here's one final skill to help you continue with these positive changes: willingness.

Getting Back to Willingness

You might recall from chapter 7 that willingness is about staying open to possibilities versus willfulness, which is when we give up, we close ourselves off and stop trying, or we do everything we can to avoid feeling something.

Everyone gets willful at times: think of a time when you gave up on your math homework, because you just couldn't figure it out, or when you were trying to talk to your parents about something, and you couldn't get them to see your perspective, so you shut down. It makes sense that sometimes you might choose not to use the skills you've been learning, because they're hard, they don't give you the same quick sense of relief that your target behavior did, it takes so much energy to change your behavior, and so on.

So here is a reminder about how to get back to a more willing place, which will increase the likelihood that you'll stay on track (or get back on track) by using skills:

1. Accept that willfulness has come up by saying to yourself, *I'm feeling willful right now.*

2. Use your skills to reregulate: do a forward bend, stick your face in cold water, and do your paced breathing (see chapter 2).

3. Change your posture and body language by using willing hands and the half smile (see chapter 7).

If you've tried these things and willfulness is still there, you can ask yourself, *What is it that I'm afraid of?* Fear or anxiety often keeps willfulness hanging around. For example, you might find it frightening to think about who you'll be if you no longer have this problem behavior; or to think about how you'll manage without it; or to think about what expectations might be put on you if you're managing better. If you can figure out what the worst thing is that you're imagining—the "what if"—this may help you move to a more willing place, where you're able to bring other skills to bear in that moment to help you be more effective. If you can figure out what you're afraid of, you may see that the threat isn't actually very realistic—in other words, you'll see that your fear doesn't fit the facts!

The good news is, you've already been practicing willingness at times, since you've just finished reading this book! I truly believe that you can make these positive changes in your life, even though it's hard, because I've seen so many people do it. Keep your focus on those long-term goals, envisioning what a life worth living looks like for you. Remember that these skills don't come with guarantees, but my experience from working with others tells me that if you put the energy and effort into learning and practicing these skills, you will make positive changes. Your work has only just begun. Your task now is to keep pushing yourself to make these changes, which will help you get to that life worth living. Envision that future. Think about your values and your goals. Imagine that life worth living. And then ask yourself the question: *Are you willing?*

References

Brantley, M., and T. Hanauer. 2008. *The Gift of Loving-Kindness.* Oakland, CA: New Harbinger Publications.

Holt-Lunstad, J., T. B. Smith, M. Baker, T. Harris, and D. Stephenson. 2015. "Loneliness and Social Isolation as Risk Factors for Mortality: A Meta-Analytic Review." *Perspectives on Psychological Science* 10 (2): 227–37.

Linehan, M. M. 1993. *Cognitive-Behavioral Treatment of Borderline Personality Disorder.* New York: Guilford Press.

———. 2005. "This One Moment: Skills for Everyday Mindfulness." *From Chaos to Freedom* video series, part 4. DVD. Seattle: Behavioral Tech.

———. 2014. *DBT Skills Training Manual.* Second edition. New York: Guilford Press.

May, G. 1982. *Will and Spirit.* New York: HarperCollins.

Van Dijk, S. 2011. *Don't Let Your Emotions Run Your Life for Teens.* Oakland, CA: New Harbinger Publications.

Sheri Van Dijk, MSW, is a mental health therapist and renowned dialectical behavior therapy (DBT) expert. She is author of seven books, including *Calming the Emotional Storm, Don't Let Your Emotions Run Your Life for Teens,* and *Relationship Skills 101 for Teens*. Her books focus on using DBT skills to help people manage their emotions and cultivate lasting well-being. She is the recipient of the R.O. Jones Award from the Canadian Psychiatric Association.

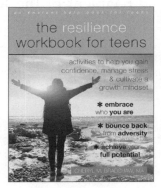
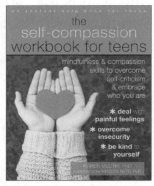

FROM OUR PUBLISHER—

As the publisher at New Harbinger and a clinical psychologist since 1978, I know that emotional problems are best helped with evidence-based therapies. These are the treatments derived from scientific research (randomized controlled trials) that show what works. Whether these treatments are delivered by trained clinicians or found in a self-help book, they are designed to provide you with proven strategies to overcome your problem.

Therapies that aren't evidence-based—whether offered by clinicians or in books—are much less likely to help. In fact, therapies that aren't guided by science may not help you at all. That's why this New Harbinger book is based on scientific evidence that the treatment can relieve emotional pain.

This is important: if this book isn't enough, and you need the help of a skilled therapist, use the following resources to find a clinician trained in the evidence-based protocols appropriate for your problem. And if you need more support—a community that understands what you're going through and can show you ways to cope—resources for that are provided below, as well.

Real help is available for the problems you have been struggling with. The skills you can learn from evidence-based therapies will change your life.

Matthew McKay, PhD
Publisher, New Harbinger Publications

If you need a therapist, the following organization can help you find a therapist trained in dialectical behavior therapy (DBT).

Behavioral Tech, LLC
please visit www.behavioraltech.org and click on *Find a DBT Therapist*.

For additional support for patients, family, and friends, please contact the following:

Anxiety and Depression Association of American (ADAA)
visit www.adaa.org

National Center for PTSD
visit www.ptsd.va.gov

National Alliance on Mental Illness (NAMI)
visit www.nami.org

Register your **new harbinger** titles for additional benefits!

When you register your **new harbinger** title—purchased in any format, from any source—you get access to benefits like the following:

- Downloadable accessories like printable worksheets and extra content

- Instructional videos and audio files

- Information about updates, corrections, and new editions

Not every title has accessories, but we're adding new material all the time.

Access free accessories in 3 easy steps:

1. Sign in at NewHarbinger.com (or **register** to create an account).

2. Click on **register a book**. Search for your title and click the **register** button when it appears.

3. Click on the **book cover or title** to go to its details page. Click on **accessories** to view and access files.

That's all there is to it!

If you need help, visit:

NewHarbinger.com/accessories

new harbinger
CELEBRATING
40 YEARS